Indira and Daisy
Rosemary Morris

Print ISBNs
Amazon print 9780228626206
Ingram Spark 9780228626213
Barnes & Noble 9780228626220

Copyright 2023 by Rosemary Morris
Cover art by Michelle Lee

All rights reserved. Without limiting the rights under copyright reserved above, no part of this publication may be reproduced, stored in or introduced into a retrieval system, or transmitted, in any form, or by any means (electronic, mechanical, photocopying, recording, or otherwise) without the prior written permission of both the copyright owner and the publisher of this book.

Dedication

*With gratitude to my friend
Indradyumna Maharaja.*

Bapuji. - Father. Govinda Nathwani.

Ba. - Mother. Kumud Nathwani.

Indira's brother. - Gopal

Dada - Paternal Grandfather. Balaram.

Kaka - Paternal Uncle. Harish Nathwani. (Mr N)

Kaki - Paternal Aunt. Pushpa Nathwani. (Mrs N)

Massie - Kumud's sister. Janavi Lakhani

Table of Contents

Part One 5
Chapter One 5
Chapter Two 20
Chapter Three 37
Chapter Four 49
Chapter Five 64
Chapter Six 77
Chapter Seven 91
Chapter Eight 104
Chapter Nine 119
Part Two 134
Chapter Ten 134
Chapter Eleven 150
Chapter Twelve 163
Chapter Thirteen 176
Chapter Fourteen 188
Bibliography 203

Part One

Chapter One
November 1982

Daisy Royston hoped Indira Nathwani would be allowed to spend Christmas with her and her mum. Eleven years after they met at nursery school, when they were three years-old, they were still best friends.

"Indira, I'm looking forward to next week when I'll stay at your house to celebrate Diwali. This year please spend Christmas with us." Daisy wriggled with excitement on her seat in the ancient, Austin the best car her mum could afford.

Indira fidgeted. "I'll stay with you if my parents agree."

Indira caught her lower lip between her teeth. Sympathetic, Daisy squeezed her friend's hand. She knew Indira longed for the freedom her mother, Julia Royston, a single mum, allowed her. "Promise to ask you mum and dad later."

"Is there a problem, Indira?" Julia asked from the driver's seat.

"N...no," Indira replied. "If I'm allowed to, I'd love to spend Christmas with you and Daisy."

"And we'd love to have you, but, of course, you must have your parents' consent. Tell you what. I'll ask them if you may join us," Julia said.

A week later, on Diwali, Indira's mum, Kumud Nathwani, picked them up from Chermister Grammar School. Daisy grinned as she dumped her heavy school bag on the floor and settled down on the luxurious back seat. She always enjoyed a ride in the BMW, so different to her mother's bumpy old car. Mrs Nathwani was very fortunate because Indira's dad gave her the car, with the personal number plate KMD 1. Some people are born lucky, Daisy reflected, but Indira's family experienced mixed fortunes. They were among fifty-thousand Asian passport holders, whom the president, Idi Amin, expelled from Uganda ten years ago in 1972. When they arrived in England, the Nathwani family struggled to make ends meet after living in the lap of luxury in Kampala. They were saved from poverty when Indira's grandfather won a fortune on the lottery. Daisy wished her hard-working mum could win one.

The car drew to a smooth halt in one of the garages at Nathwani's large timber-framed house in the most exclusive part of Cherminster. "Hurry up girls," Kumud said. "There's lots to do."

Excitement, like the bubbles of the champagne her mother had allowed her to taste at a wedding, fizzed through her. For the first time she would spend a night in the eight-bedroom, detached house, which had several bathrooms, attics, a large cellar, and immaculate front and back gardens maintained by a gardener and located in the most exclusive part of Chermister. The council house, one of a terrace she and her mum lived in at the lower end of town, only had a tiny garden in which they grew a rose bush, flowers, and vegetables. She wished it were larger and backed onto a large park like the one behind Indira's home.

Indira stood on the doorstep. Her expression anxious, she looked up at dark blue-grey clouds. "Diwali will be ruined if it rains."

"But we'll be indoors, won't we?" Daisy asked.

"Yes," Indira's mum said as she opened the front door. "Hurry upstairs, girls. Please shower quickly and change your clothes. I want you to help me while we wait for the men to come home."

Daisy knew better than to walk across the thick cream-coloured carpet in the hall wearing her shoes. She took them off and put them side by side on a shelf in the shoe rack. After years of visiting the Nathwani's, it seemed as natural not to wear outdoor shoes in their house as it did to brush her teeth every day.

Indira lingered at the foot of the stairs. "Ba, it's lovely having Daisy here for Diwali. May I spend Christmas with her?"

"If your bapuj agrees." Ba shook her forefinger at her. "Don't start arguing with me and take that sulky look off your face. Now please get changed."

Daisy frowned. Although Indira didn't answer back, she knew her friend was upset. What was the problem? Why couldn't Indira's mother say 'yes, of course you may?' Why was it up to Indira's father?

In Indira's large bedroom decorated in pink and white, Daisy put her suitcase down, and resisted the temptation to stroke velvet the colour of pink sugared almonds that upholstered the window seats and a pair of chairs. She looked up. For heaven's sake! Instead of a shade around a single bulb, a crystal chandelier hung from the ceiling. At home, her clever mum had sanded and varnished her bedroom furniture from the junk shop to make it look as good as new and covered her bed with a beautiful, secondhand patchwork. Nevertheless, looking at Indira's luxurious bedroom, she suppressed the twinge of the green-eyed monster which seemed disloyal to her mum who did her best to provide for them.

Indira pointed at one of the twin beds with pale pink satin bedspreads. At the end of each one lay pink toweling bath robes and piles of neatly folded towels. Too much pink? Maybe, but Indira was lucky to have a large loving family, who lived together and had oodles of money. Ashamed of her jealousy. Daisy shrugged. She wouldn't swap her mother, who loved her to bits, for anyone else in the world. However, as Grandma used to say, "Money might be the root of all evil, but give me some of it." Daisy forced her mind away from her late grandmother who she missed so much that remembering her brought tears to her eyes. She blinked, wishing Grandma was still alive, then looked at Indira. "Do you think your ba and bapuj will let you come to us for Christmas?"

Oh, I've learned so many Gujrati words that I didn't say your father and mother.

"Maybe," Indira said, her tone of voice sharp as a carving knife while she took off her green and gold striped school tie.

Curious, Daisy scrutinised her friend's face. Possibly, the Nathwanis didn't think her home was good enough for their daughter to stay in. "My mum said you may come on Christmas Eve and stay with us for three nights. Of course, our house is very small, but you would be comfortable sleeping in my bedroom."

"I'm sure I would." Indira took off her school uniform and collected a bathrobe and large towel. "Let's get a move on. My mother and aunt need our help."

While Indira showered in the ensuite, Daisy picked up a sari from one of the bedroom chairs. She draped one end of the feather light, pale gold silk embroidered with gold, and intertwined with silver, over her head. She peeped into a full-length mirror. "I'd like to wear one," she murmured. Her reflection stared back at her when Indira startled her as she entered the bedroom.

"I wondered what I'd look like in a sari," Daisy explained, aware that she blushed although she hadn't done anything wrong, had she?

"You would look gorgeous." Indira sat at her dressing table and combed her lustrous, thick, black hair which was long enough to sit on.

Daisy tried to refold the sari, failed, and put it in a small heap on the chair. She picked up the robe and a towel from the end of her bed. In the bathroom with a pink-veined marble floor, awestruck by the expensive decor and fragrant toiletries, she showered quickly.

In the bedroom she smiled at Indira dressed in a turquoise blue top printed on the front with an image of mother and baby dolphin, and the logo, Save the Dolphins. "You look nice. I hope you really like the top," Daisy said. She had saved her pocket money to buy it and given it to Indira on her fourteenth birthday and chosen it because of her own interest in Green Peace and environmental issues.

Indira squeezed a pair of gold bangles over her hands onto her wrist. "Yes, I love the colour. I wouldn't wear it if I didn't like it."

Reassured by the expression in her friend's large mahogany brown eyes, Daisy put on her underwear. She adjusted her bra, pulled on a favourite pair of faded denim jeans, and a secondhand sky-blue jumper she bought the previous week from a charity shop. A quick glance in a full-length mirror confirmed the jeans were too short because she had shot up in recent months. She sighed. Mum never had quite enough money, so she didn't want to ask her for a new pair. Perhaps she could find a pair in a secondhand shop to buy with her pocket money.

Had Indira noticed she had outgrown the jeans? "Mum bought me a new dress in a sale to wear on Christmas day. What will you wear to celebrate with us? One of your gorgeous Indian outfits, a sari, or western clothes?"

Her friend squared her shoulders while she put her dirty school clothes and underwear in a pretty laundry basket with pink ruffles around the rim. "You don't understand!" Her face averted Indira hurried towards the bedroom door.

Daisy looked in the mirror to check she looked tidy. Hurt, because she had believed she and Indira kept no secrets from each other, she tweaked a curl before she spoke. "What don't I understand?"

Indira turned around. "Oh, nothing."

Were there tears in Indira's large eyes? Surely not. What did her friend have to cry about? She didn't have to watch her mother struggle to save money for rainy days that came too often.

Her slippers sank into the deep pile of the carpet as she followed her friend out onto the landing. They linked arms as they went down the broad stairs. On the ground floor, she gazed at the three feet wide, two feet long wall hangings with geometric designs formed by small beads as brightly coloured as gemstones stitched onto a background of white beads. She pointed at them. "When I grow up and have my own place, I want door hangings like those."

"Do you? My kaki thinks they are old-fashioned, but my Dada likes them and as the eldest member of the family he has the final say about everything." She patted Daisy's arm with her free hand. "If you still like them when you move out of your mum's house, I'll ask Bapuji to order some for you from India."

"Would your father really do that?"

Indira nodded.

"Perhaps we could share a place."

Indira's long black eyelashes veiled her eyes. "Who knows what will happen in the future?"

Unexpectedly, Indira laughed as she gestured to a rosewood corner table with a marble top. "I suppose you would also like to have a bronze statue of Ganesh?"

"Yes, I would." Why did her friend seem so sad? "Do you and your family really believe that if you worship him, he will remove all obstacles?"

"Kaki worships Ganesh, but the rest of us don't although we respect him. We worship Lord Krishna, who, as you know, we believe is God."

Daisy looked at the well-polished figure the size of an average three-year-old. Ganesh had become such a familiar sight that she no longer found his elephant head and round belly with a deep navel strange. She was also surprised because, for the first time, she appreciated the twinkle in his painted eyes. "If something's bothering you, Indira, ask Ganesh to help you,"

"I don't think he would."

"Try. He might amaze you, or you could ask Krishna. Before she died, my grandma said faith in God can move mountains." She smiled at the statue.

Would Ganesh help Mum if she asked him to? Shame heated her cheeks. Such a thought would have horrified her grandma, who had attended church every Sunday and taken her to Sunday school when she was little. She had respected the ten Commandments, one of which was thou shalt not bow down before graven images.

But was the figure of Ganesh one? Grandma would have said yes. Daisy considered it was merely an interesting statue and she would not bow down to anyone or anything.

Indira said something. "I beg your pardon. What did you say?" Daisy asked, dragged out of her thoughts.

"I said I'm hungry. Let's see what there is for tea." At the end of the hall, Indira opened the door to the dining room and beckoned to her.

Daisy sniffed the delicious aromas of incense, flowers, and sandalwood from the half-open door of the temple-room, and ones from the kitchen. Her tummy rumbled. Afternoon tea in the Nathwani household would be as substantial as every other meal served. She must curb her appetite. If she ate too much, she wouldn't have room to enjoy the Diwali feast.

Kumud put a steel plate piled high with deep fried triangular samosas made with pastry stuffed with spiced potatoes and peas, which Daisy knew Indira's grandfather, Balaram, had offered with other teatime snacks to the family's deities, statues of Krishna carved from black marble and Radha carved from white marble.

"Sit at the table in the dining room, girls," Mrs N, Indira's Aunt Pushpa, said.

Seated, Daisy couldn't control her giggles.

A frown appeared on the lady's forehead while she adjusted the end of the sari which covered her head. "What's funny, Daisy?" She waited for an answer while she served them with gattia and sev, snacks made from spiced dough pressed through different sized sieves into macaroni, spaghetti, or vermicelli widths, then fried until they became pale gold and as crunchy as crisps.

"I remembered the day when I said the lentil soup – what-do-you-call it, oh yes, toor dhal, smelled nice and-"

"And Ba threw it away," Indira interrupted.

"Yes, until your mother told me, how was I to know smelling food counts as tasting, and your family doesn't eat anything which has not first been offered to your god, Krishna, to enjoy," Daisy said.

"I'll never forget it," Mrs N said. "When my husband asked me to serve him some dhal, Daisy's face turned as pink as the tip of a petal of the flower she's named for."

Fortunately, Indira's mum also saw the funny side of it and laughed.

"I'll bring the tea," Mrs N called from the kitchen.

Daisy hoped it wouldn't be masala tea. She didn't like the brew of sugar, tea leaves and milk with cloves, cardamom, cinnamon, ginger and freshly milled black pepper boiled with water and milk.

"Which kind of tea have you made, Kaki?" Indira asked when her aunt brought a tray on which were two teapots.

"Masala tea for us and plain tea for your little friend," Mrs N said.

Daisy frowned. Not so little, I'm nearly fifteen. I wish she wouldn't speak to me and Indira as though we are still small children.

Mrs N's smile softened her angular features. "You should drink masala tea, Daisy. The spices would help to keep you free from coughs and colds."

Daisy kept quiet because it would be rude to insist that she really didn't like the taste. Instead, she smiled back at her friend's aunt, whom she always addressed as Mrs N.

The tray seemed too heavy for the thin lady. Daisy stood and went to help her.

"Thank you, you are very kind, but I can manage." Mrs N put the tray on the table and transferred the contents onto it. "Please be seated and serve yourself."

Daisy helped herself with some of her favourite tomato chutney and a dollop of bitter-sweet tamarind chutney to eat with discs of thin sliced potatoes coated with gram flour batter and then deep fried.

"Ba, what do you want us to do when we've finished our tea?" Indira asked brusquely.

Puzzled, Daisy looked at her friend, whose family's harmony fascinated her, though she sometimes suspected there were ripples beneath the tranquil atmosphere in their home. But she never questioned her friend about them. Instead, she enjoyed their hospitality and admired the beautiful house.

"Indira and Daisy, I want you to put candles in jars," Indira's mother said. "If it stops raining, we'll stand them along the edges of the paths in the front and back gardens."

"You'll light the candles to celebrate the return of the divine couple Rama and Sita to their kingdom after Rama was exiled, won't you?" Daisy asked to make sure she understood the custom.

"Yes, Daisy, as I said, if it stops raining."

Indira's grandfather had told her the romantic story of the God Rama, who set the example as the perfect husband and king, and his eternal consort, the Goddess Sita, whom a demon stole while they were in exile.

"I hope Sita, the Goddess of Fortune, will bless all of us this year," Mrs Nathwani said.

How sad Indira's aunt looked. Probably because, as Indira had once told her, Mrs N longed to have a baby. Perhaps she would pray for one.

"What else do you want me to do, Ba?"

"Clear the table, Indira, before you arrange the candles. When you've done that, spread the white cloths over the floor of the lounge for everyone to sit on."

"What about the furniture, Ba?"

"Before your father and uncle went to work this morning, they pushed all of it back against the wall."

Daisy picked up the empty teapots and put them on the tray.

Mrs N's hands fluttered. "No, no, put them down. You're our guest. Indira will clear up."

Daisy smiled. "I'd like to help." Mrs N opened her mouth to protest again, but before she could do so, Daisy continued. "All of you are kind. You've always made me feel like one of your family." She glanced at her friend, who was busy putting dirty plates and mugs onto another tray. "I hope Indira will feel at home when she comes to us for Christmas."

Neither Mrs Nathwani nor talkative Mrs N said a word. Daisy frowned. Had she said something wrong? "The least I can do is to carry a few things to the kitchen," she said made uncomfortable by the silence.

Indira eyed her mother and aunt.

Puzzled because neither lady acknowledged her comment about the proposed visit, Daisy carried the tray to the kitchen.

"After I put the food away, we might as well load the dishwasher," Indira said when they finished clearing the table.

Indira rinsed everything and Daisy put it into the machine, wondering why Indira hunched her shoulders. However, plump, good-natured Mrs Nathwani didn't seem to notice how anxious Indira seemed when she bustled into the kitchen.

"Oh, thank you girls, for clearing up. Too good of you to help, Daisy. Indira, I suggest you wear your green sari embroidered with peacocks, this evening."

"Not my mauve one with-" Indira began.

"No," Mrs Nathwani's warned her daughter not to argue. "What about you, Daisy? I hope you have something nice to wear."

She nodded, hoping Mrs Nathwani would approve of the ankle-length, cotton turquoise dress she bought in a charity shop at the posh end of Cherminster, but possibly it was unsuitable. She took a deep breath before she spoke. "Mrs Nathwani, you and Mrs N always look so beautiful in your lovely saris that I wish I had one instead of a dress."

Kumud clapped her hands. "I'll give you one."

Her cheeks hot with embarrassment, Daisy twirled a strand of her hair around her forefinger. "No, no, I could not accept it, I only want to borrow one."

"Don't worry about it, Daisy," Indira tried to reassure her. "You would be doing her a favour. Ba hoards more new saris than we can wear. Bapuji pretends to disapprove of her extravagance. He says that if he's ever bankrupt, he can make another fortune by selling her saris and gold jewelry."

"Your family are so kind and generous that I hope we can repay them during Christmas," Daisy said.

Chapter Two

Daisy and Indira held opposite ends of white cloths. One by one they spread them over the carpet in the drawing room. After putting beeswax candles in jars on windowsills, they went upstairs to Indira's bedroom.

"Ooh, for me?" Daisy looked at the delphinium-blue, silk sari, matching blouse, and blue cotton petticoat at the foot of the guest bed.

"Ooh," she repeated. Her mum would like the fabulous material as much as she did.

Indira removed her emerald-green sari from a cupboard. "Ba took you seriously when you asked to wear a sari. I hope you weren't joking."

"No, I wasn't. For ages, I've wanted to wear a sari."

"Well then, I'll show you how to put it on."

Surprised by Indira's cross voice, Daisy stared at her. "What's wrong? Why are you grumpy this evening? Have I upset you? Do you want me to go home?"

Indira sighed and shook her head. "You haven't. Sorry for being so-" her voice trailed away before she added. "Of course, I don't want you to go home. I want you to enjoy the Diwali celebrations."

"Something's wrong, Indira. What is it? Please tell me. I won't repeat it to anyone else."

"You wouldn't understand." Indira wiped her eyes on the back of her hand.

"What wouldn't I understand?" Her best friend lived in the lap of luxury with her loving family. Why was she miserable?

"How I feel."

"Explain it, Indira. I might be able to help."

"I'm sorry for being irritable. Forget what I said," Indira said.

"I can't. We've always been best mates, able to confide in each other."

Indira shrugged. "Things change. We're still best friends but we're growing up. I'm nearly fifteen, no longer a child."

"I know, but why are you upset?" Daisy persisted.

"Forget it. I was being foolish." Indira's smile did not alter the sad expression in her eyes. "We must change before my father and uncle come home."

Daisy put on the short-sleeved blouse that left her midriff bare, then slipped the floor length cotton petticoat over her head. She held it in place with both hands at her waist.

"Tie the drawstrings tightly toward the right, Daisy."

"How can you be sure it will fit me?"

"Saris are wide and long enough to be suitable for everyone."

"How can they be?"

They're adjusted by tucking the upper edge in at the waist. Short ladies like Pushpa Kaki tuck more in at the waist than taller ladies."

Indira shook out Daisy's sari, found the top right-hand corner and tucked it into the petticoat between the line of Daisy's right hip and belly button. "You've tied the petticoat tightly enough to prevent the sari from falling down," Indira said, as she tucked it around the petticoat into the waistband. She brought the other end around Daisy's back, under her right armpit and over her left shoulder. "Excellent. It's long enough to either hang to the back of your knees or drape over your head."

Daisy looked down at a loop of surplus material. "What about that?"

"You'll see." Indira stood behind her, put her arms around her waist, pleated the excess silk, and tucked it in at the waistband, then stood in front of her to check that the pleats hung properly.

Daisy giggled nervously. "I'm afraid the sari will fall down if I move."

"It won't, but I'll pin the pleats in place at the waist." Indira fetched a large safety pin, thrust the pointed end through the petticoat and sari and fastened it.

"Do you and your mother and aunt keep your saris in place with safety pins?"

"No, we're used to wearing them."

"I'm surprised, because although I'm wrapped up like a parcel, the sari is featherlight. Do I look nice?" Daisy asked anxiously.

"Gorgeous, look in the mirror and see for yourself."

Daisy looked at her reflection in a mirror on a door of the fitted wardrobe. Did she know the girl looking back at her? One completely different to her everyday self. In the traditional clothes which the Nathwani ladies always wore, had she become another person? "Don't be silly," she whispered too low for Indira to hear her and admired the sari, as blue as her eyes, and pink embroidery and sequins the colour of her cheeks. She twirled around several times and glimpsed the reflection of her thick, waist-length, wavy, blonde hair fanning out. Satisfied with her appearance, she looked at her friend. "And you look beautiful, but you always do, even in school uniform." She paused for a moment to appreciate her friend's oval face, large eyes, long lashes, and a cupid's bow mouth with dimples on each side.

Indira laughed. "In boring school uniform?"

"I'm not beautiful, but Mum says you are and that you always stand out in a crowd."

Indira opened the bedroom door. "Time to go downstairs."

In the hall, Daisy gazed at Indira's mother, dressed in turquoise-blue silk chiffon sari embroidered with gold thread, and decorated with sequins. Indira must be an image of her mother at the same age. No wonder she had received an offer to star in a film. "You are beautiful," Daisy said with genuine appreciation.

"It's kind of you to say so."

"It is true. And thank you for lending me this lovely sari."

A smile rippled across Mrs Nathwani's face. "No, no, Daisy, it's not a loan. It is a Diwali gift."

"Oh, no, I'm sure it's too expensive for me to accept," Daisy said, embarrassed because she had not brought Diwali gifts.

"Think nothing of it." Mrs Nathwani looked around. "Where's Indira?"

"I don't know. I thought she followed me downstairs."

Before Indira's mother could say anything else, the front door opened, and Mr Nathwani entered the hall, took off his coat and hung it up on the coat rack. "Goodness gracious me, who is this lovely young lady?" he teased and looked affectionately at his wife. "Please introduce us."

Daisy smiled at the tall, handsome man, his skin the colour of wheat, his thin lips that often curved, as they did now, in a smile, and clear, chestnut brown, observant eyes. Looking at him dressed in a well-cut grey suit, she wished she remembered her own father. "Mr Nathwani," she protested, "you know who I am."

"Are you, can you be Daisy?"

She nodded and giggled.

"I'm sorry for not recognising you at first because you look like a princess." He turned toward his wife. "But where is my very own princess?"

"Here I am, Bapuji," Indira said from the stairs.

Mr Nathwani beamed as Indira stepped down them toward him, the emeralds set in her gold earrings, necklace and nose ring sparkling by the light of the crystal chandelier.

Again, the green-eyed monster, jealousy, which her grandmother had warned her against, surfaced. Indira was lucky. Her father's face lit up like a Christmas candle whenever he looked at her.

Daisy sighed. Would my dad have looked at me as lovingly as Indira's dad looks at her? Twenty-six was too young for him to have died.

"Bapuji."

"Yes, Indira."

"Daisy's mum invited me to spend Christmas with them. Please say I may."

Indira's Uncle Harish, a head shorter than his older brother stepped into the hall and removed his cashmere coat, which his wife hurried to hang up.

Indira tilted her chin, her large eyes raging with inner fire. "Bapuji, please say I may go to Daisy's on Christmas Eve and come home on the twenty-seventh."

"We'll see what your Dada has to say about it. Where is he?"

"Dressing the deities in their new outfits," Mrs N explained.

Indira's mother stepped forward. "Don't pester your father and grandfather about the invitation." She fetched a box of matches and tapers. "It's dusk. Shall we go outside with Daisy and your aunt to help me to light the Diwali candles?"

"I'm glad it stopped raining. The garden looks like fairyland," Daisy said later as she admired the magical effect of dancing candlelight on the steps, the paths, and the patio. Indoors, her impression intensified when Mrs Nathwani and Mrs N lit candles on all the windowsills and turned off the electric lights.

"Surely the Goddess of Fortune will pass over our house, see the candlelight indoors and out, and bless us." Kumud stroked Indira's back. "I wonder what she will make of my silly daughter."

Did she say Indira was silly because she wanted to accept the invitation to celebrate Christmas?

Mrs Nathwani looked at the clock. "Six o' clock. Your brother should be home."

"Perhaps he missed his train." Daisy looked forward to seeing Gopal, the most handsome young man she had ever seen, with his mother and Indira's wheat coloured skin, black curly hair, and his father and grandfather's height.

His mother frowned. "Since he started his course in Business Studies and Law in London, he's always late coming home. Sometimes he eats out instead of returning home to have dinner."

Daisy sensed that although she loved her daughter, her twenty-one-year-old son, would always be more important to her. Sorry for her friend, she remembered a puzzling remark made by Indira's aunt a couple of years ago. "My niece isn't really a part of our family. She's part of her future husband's family."

The Nathwanis have peculiar beliefs. If I get married nothing will stop Mum and me from still belonging to each other. She had no time to think any more about it. Guests were arriving to celebrate Rama and Sita's return to Ayodhya, their capital city.

Daisy heard the conch shell, which always struck a thrilling chord in her, announce the beginning of the service. She hurried into the marble-floored temple room where worship commenced with songs of praise after which flowers, money, food, and drinks would be offered to Krishna and his consort Radha Rani.

With a twinkle in his eyes, Indira's grandfather had explained, "Christians ask their heavenly father to provide their daily bread. We offer God food before we eat."

Puzzled, she had said, "But you have more than one god."

"Ah, you are confused. We believe Krishna is supreme. Sometimes he takes birth as Lord Rama or in other forms who we worship. Like a prime minister who assigns tasks to cabinet ministers, He delegates jobs to demi-gods. He also sends his representatives to earth with specific roles, among whom, I believe are Lord Jesus Christ and Mohammed," he explained and smiled at her.

"Is that what every Hindu believes?"

"Ah," he had repeated. "You are a clever child. Hindu is the name the Muslim invaders gave to the nation when they crossed the River Indus. Some Hindus worship demi-gods, but my family doesn't, we are Vaishnavas, which means we worship Lord Krishna, who we accept as The Supreme Person."

His explanations are always interesting, Daisy thought when she stood on the left-hand side of the temple room next to Indira with the ladies and children. Although she did not think of herself as religious, she could not resist the beautiful oil painting of Rama and Sita in front of the altar, decorated with a flower garland; and she admired the tall marble figures of Krishna with a peacock feather tucked into his turban, and a flute in his hand, and Radharani, with fragrant garlands of flowers.

"Their clothes are new," Indira whispered. "My Dada ordered them from India."

Daisy admired the jade green silk outfits embroidered with padded lotus flowers. She opened her mouth to murmur, 'their clothes are fabulous,' when Indira nudged her. "Come and offer them some flower petals."

Daisy copied her friend, who took a handful from a silver tray held by Mrs Nathwani, then put a few at the feet of each of each statue. She didn't want to imagine what her grandmother would say if she looked down at her from heaven.

Balaram blew the conch shell to announce the ceremonies were over. Again, the loud, hollow sound sent a shiver down her spine. The turquoise-blue velvet curtains in front of the altar closed. Appreciative of sandalwood incense, she followed the crowd of guests into the sitting room where everyone sat down and chatted while waiting to enjoy the Diwali feast. She wished Indira could sit next to her, but she was busy serving sweet rice simmered with sugar, flaked almonds, and raisins.

Daisy heard Indira's grandfather say her name to a lady sitting near her as he ladled a portion of cauliflower, peas, potato curry onto her plate. Her mouth watered so much that it seemed as though she had already bitten into the spongy cheese that had absorbed the delicious flavour of tomatoes and spices.

She smiled at the tall old gentleman with silver-white hair, dressed in a long white cotton tunic and trousers, who she liked very much. "Thank you. What did you say about me to that lady in the purple and green sari?"

"I told her you're Indira's friend, and that I'm sure Lord Rama and Lady Sita are pleased by your presence on this auspicious occasion." He moved on to serve the lady who sat on her right.

Did his words imply some guests thought a European should not be at the celebration? She frowned as she looked down at her plate, and then looked up at Indira's uncle, who served her with chickpeas cooked with tomatoes, chilies, and spice.

"My father's right, Daisy. You look so beautiful in your sari that I'm sure Lord Rama and Lady Sita had a delightful surprise when you offered them flowers; and that Lord Krishna is pleased to see you. He is every living entity's friend, and even knows their past, present, and future."

Daisy blushed, not at the compliment, but because her tummy rumbled with hunger. She didn't need to worry. The embarrassing sound could not have been heard above the high-pitched conversations made by over forty guests sitting in four rows, the men in two, the ladies, dressed in brightly coloured saris, and children in the others.

She shivered, despite the warmth from the central heating increased by so many people. Was it true that Krishna knew what would happen to her in the future?

Mrs N served thin, round flat breads called chapattis. Mrs Nathwani served her with her favourite Indian sweet, gulab jamans, round, brown balls made with milk powder soaked in sugar syrup. Indira, who had served the sweet rice, ladled salted yoghurt mixed with grated cucumber on Daisy's large metal plate. Someone she didn't know put rice next to the curry and another lady ladled lentil dahl, a spiced soup onto it.

Everyone chanted a prayer, which Daisy knew thanked God for the food they were about to eat, then tucked in. Everything looked so scrumptious that Daisy did not know what to taste first. She broke off a piece of chapatti with her right hand, used it to scoop up curry and popped it into her mouth. The meals here were always delicious. Today it tasted heavenly.

"Are you liking our food?" the plump lady seated next to her asked.

"I love it, if it's not chili hot."

The lady's gold bangles tinkled as she gesticulated. "Chili is good for the digestion."

Daisy smiled. "That's what Mrs Nathwani says."

"It's true. Even if they make your mouth burn."

"Thank you, I'll remember it," Daisy said. She ate engrossed in the meal, the scents, and the buzz of conversation.

When the last guest could eat no more, the family and others who had served ate quickly. After the dishes were cleared away, everyone went into the garden to watch the fireworks.

Gopal, who arrived at the beginning of the temple service, gave her a sparkler. "Be careful. You don't want to set your sari on fire."

Daisy held it at arm's length. She loved the effect of the silver sparks that shone so brightly before they died against night's dark backdrop.

Indira took a sparkler from her brother, circled it around and around until it died. She faced him. "Gopal, would you talk to Dada, Bapuji, and Kaka for me?"

"About what? Are you planning mischief?" he asked, his voice sharp.

"No. Please persuade them to allow me to spend Christmas at Daisy's house."

His arched eyebrows drew together. He spoke after hesitating for a moment or two. "I will, but, as you should know by now, I can't influence them where you're concerned."

"Please try, Mum and I really want Indira to enjoy herself with us," Daisy said, admiring Gopal's thick hair swept back from his forehead and his large dark eyes with long eyelashes any girl would envy.

Gopal gazed into her eyes. "Daisy, to please you and Indira, I'll try, but I am sure that by now you should know what my parents are like where their princess is concerned."

* * *

"What did Gopal mean when he said I should know what your parents are like where their princess is concerned?" Daisy asked later while she and Indira got ready for bed.

"You wouldn't understand, Daisy," Indira said, her voice muffled as she pulled her pajama top over her head. Seated on the edge of her bed, Indira hunched her back, drew her knees up to her chin, and linked her arms around them.

"Indira, my grandma said that a trouble shared is a trouble halved. Please tell me what the problem is. I'll help you if I can," Daisy said while she brushed her hair.

"Although you've been visiting us for years, there's so much you don't understand. I'll spell it out for you. My brother meant that I'm an Indian girl born into a family from Gujarat whose family is Vaisnavas."

"Vaisnavas?"

"Vaisnavas believe Sri Krishna is God. Anyway, my family think of me as their princess, who must follow all the conventions and obey them without question. Surely you know by now that the men's decisions are law in this household."

"I've never thought about it, but I suppose I do." Daisy put the hairbrush down. She turned around on the dressing table stool to face her friend. "What has that to do with my mum's invitation?"

Indira sniffed. "I'm not allowed any freedom, not even to decide if I'll spend Christmas with you. If they could dictate how many times I breathe every minute, they would."

"It's ridiculous," Daisy said sympathetically.

"Not from their point of view. My family enjoy each other's company and that of other members of our Lohana community. They're afraid that if I go out without one of them, I'll either do something they don't approve of or something bad will happen to me."

"That's ridiculous," Daisy repeated. "I've been safe popping down to the corner shop and back since I was seven or eight years old. As for going into town alone or with friends, my mum trusts me to behave. Your family should trust you."

"Yes, they should, but to be fair, they are afraid. Gopal was attacked by a racist and they fear I might be."

"Why didn't you tell me that?" Shocked, Daisy twisted a strand of hair around her finger.

"It was a verbal attack that hurt his feelings, but it could have been worse."

"That's terrible. Poor Gopal."

Indira sighed. "If I go to university, they will be proud of me but insist I study near enough to live at home. When I pass my final exams, they will expect me to live with them until I marry." She pressed her face against her knees. "Sometimes it seems as if they are suffocating me." Indira caught her lower lip between her teeth. "I don't think that one day your mum would object to you leaving home to live at your own place. My parents would never agree to that."

Daisy frowned. Indira's life with a large loving family was not as great as she had believed. Anyway, she wouldn't swap her mum for anyone, and she would always do her best not to disappoint her. Should she be sorry for her friend? "Indira," she began, "when you're eighteen you can please yourself. Your family couldn't prevent you from moving out."

"That's true, but it would hurt them too much. They really do enjoy spending time with me, love me and expect me to spend all my spare time with them."

"Why?"

Indira sat up straight. "They don't trust anyone else to look after me. That's why they haven't agreed to let me spend Christmas with you."

"I don't want to be rude, but it's silly of them. Mum would take very good care of you. I'll ask her to have a word with them."

Indira clenched her fists. "I really want to join you for Christmas, but although I'll be angry if my parents refuse, there's nothing I can do about it. After my Dada, Bapuji, and Kaka make their minds up about something, nothing will change it. That's the way they are, and they expect me to accept their decision."

"Don't your mother and aunt have a say?"

"They can disagree, but they are not allowed to make the final decision."

Daisy yawned, stretched, and got into bed. She understood her friend bitterly resented the restrictions imposed on her. One day, Indira's temper would erupt like a volcano and her relationship with her family and community would be ruptured.

In future she would remember she had not believed something tragic would happen.

Chapter Three

Indira stretched and yawned. If she had not realised it was the first day of the Hindu New Year, she would have gone back to sleep. She smiled, looking forward to the celebrations, and glanced at the clock on the bedside table. A quarter past seven, time to get dressed.

"Daisy are you awake?" she asked quietly. No reply. Should she wake her friend? No, they had a day off from school.

By now Dada would be conducting the daily morning service, which she usually attended. Indira swung her legs over the edge of her bed. For a moment, she was tempted to go to the temple room, but it would be unacceptable to enter it dressed in her pajamas and dressing gown.

If she hurried to shower and dress, she would be in time to hear Dada reading from the Bhagavadgita, the beautiful Gita Govinda, The Song of God. No matter how many times she listened to him recite it, neither the first verses about Krishna persuading the warrior, Arjuna, to engage in the battle in which good triumphed over evil, nor any others ever bored her.

If she had the opportunity, while the curtains were closed in front of the altar, she would ask Dada to tell Bapuj and Kaka to allow her to accept Mrs Royston's invitation.

New Year's Day, Indira thought, several times, and began a new account book. This year she would be allowed more freedom. Though being able to do as she pleased would be welcome, she could not imagine life apart from her loving family.

Indira stepped out of the shower, dried herself, and put on a bathrobe. She partially dried her hip-length hair, brushed, plaited it, and secured the end with a ribbon, and put the towel and her pajamas in the large, wicker Ali Baba shaped laundry basket.

As she dressed in a new jade green sari printed with tiny multicoloured flowers, she tried to be optimistic. Who knew what would happen this year? Daisy's mum might persuade Dada, Bapuji, and Kaka to let her spend Christmas at the Royston's house. She looked at her reflection in the mirror, admiring her sari and matching blouse. Her mother, who chose all their clothes, really did have good taste. She had so much to be grateful for. Although her friend never complained, her mum could only afford to buy Daisy a few new clothes. Indira couldn't imagine being forced to search for bargains in charity shops and jumble sales.

She opened the bedroom door, shut it quietly behind her and saw her mother who was about to enter the bedroom. "Happy

New Year, Ba." Joyous, she stooped to touch her mother's feet and receive her blessing. Before she could, Ba clasped her arms and drew her upright.

"Happy New Year, Indira, but why are you whispering?"

"I don't want to wake Daisy." She looked at her mother's new vibrant yellow silk sari woven with a pattern of embroidered vine leaves and flowers. "You are beautiful, Ba."

Flustered like a young girl who received a rare compliment, Ba adjusted her gold necklace and covered her lustrous hair with the end of her sari. "Beautiful! An old woman like me?"

Indira chuckled. No one knew better than she did how much trouble Ba took when she selected the new clothes, which in accordance with custom, they wore on New Year's Day. "You were only sixteen when you married, so you are not very old. Bapuji thinks you're beautiful. I've often heard him call you Champuri."

"Yes, well, he's very kind to flatter me," Ba said.

Amused, she smiled. Ba is blushing because I said Bapuji calls her Beauty. He's right. Her face is almost smooth as a young girl' and her eyes are shining. "And, because he loves you, Ba, he also calls you pyari, his darling."

Still blushing, Ba glanced at her Rolex watch. "Oh dear, by now, your grandfather will be waiting for us in the lounge with the rest of the family."

Too late to speak in private to Dada about Christmas. It was for the best. If he refused, Indira feared that her exasperation, caused by refusal to permit her to do the simple things her school friends enjoyed, would erupt in a torrent of anger like molten lava. What harm would it do if she went to town at the weekends to meet her friends, go to the cinema or browse in shops? Envying Daisy, whose mother trusted her not to do anything foolish, Indira clenched her fists.

"Hurry up," Ba urged.

Head bowed she followed her mother downstairs while she tried to make sense of her disordered thoughts. Yesterday evening, out of loyalty and the family solidarity she had defended and explained her family's outlook on life to Daisy but -

Ba opened the sitting room door.

Indira looked at Dada. Fear clutched her. During the last year, he sometimes took a deep breath and put his hand over his heart. It frightened her. Today, he was in good health as he stood facing the family who stood facing him.

Indira took her place beside Ba and Kaki. She gazed at the men, who looked very distinguished in their new clothes. Dada, Bapuji, and Kaka, shorter than his father or brother, whose skin was several shades darker, didn't smile as often as them. Nevertheless, his posture erect, he looked equally handsome in the white tunics with long sleeves and white dhotis, lengths of cotton cloth around their waists pleated in the front and reaching the floor. Her exceptionally handsome brother, who moved with the natural grace of a big cat, had compromised like most young men of his generation. He wore a white shirt with long sleeves, without cuffs, and a band at the neck, and trousers instead of traditional clothes.

Dada's long, wide Kashmir chaddar, which Daisy called a shawl, was folded into an oblong. In front, it hung from his right shoulder to his waist and at the back to his hip. If Dada felt chilly, he would unfold the soft fabric and drape it elegantly around him.

Bapuji, his face illuminated by love, stepped forward. Out of respect for his father, and to receive his blessings, he touched her grandfather's feet, then stood upright. Grandfather drew him up into a close embrace. They wished each other Happy New Year and Dada popped a piece of burfi, a fudge-like sweetmeat made from sweetened, homemade condensed milk, into Bapuji's mouth, and then gave him an envelope which contained money.

Her father stepped back, and Ba, her hair covered by the end of her sari approached Dada. A beautiful picture of humility she touched his feet, then straightened. After they exchanged the seasonal greeting, he put a piece of burfi into her mouth then an envelope into her right hand.

Kaka observed the custom. Dada embraced him, fed him with burfi and gave him an envelope. Kaki took her husband's place. Her expression guarded she quickly observed the custom. Had anyone else noticed the sheen of tears in her eyes, which Indira guessed were because she hoped her saintly father-in-law's blessings would fulfil her longing to have a baby. Gopal took her place. With a smile he paid his respects straightened, received blessings, burfi and an envelope, and hugged Dada.

Next, she paid her respects to Dada, then Gopal paid them to their parents. turned to pay them to her father. About to touch Bapuji's feet, Indira turned her head to see what her brother was staring at.

Daisy! Dressed in pajamas, her hair a riot of untidy curls, her feet bare, stood at the threshold. For how long had she been watching them? Her eyes glittered, her mouth was shaped like an O, and her nostrils screwed up. How could she explain to her friend the old-age custom of paying respects and receiving blessings from senior members of the family?

Her cheeks hot, Indira stood still.

"Indira, your father is waiting," prompted Ba who stood with her back to Daisy and, obviously, had not noticed her.

Reluctant to observe the custom in Daisy's presence, Indira hesitated.

"No, no," Bapuji protested. "Don't force my princess to touch my feet if she doesn't want to."

In some Hindu families, daughters never touched their elders' feet because they were considered members of their future husbands and in-laws' family. Her mind raced. Was that how her father thought of her?

Embarrassed by her friend's presence, Indira wanted to take her upstairs to get ready for the day, to prevent her witnessing her touch Bapuji's feet, but he might be hurt if she didn't make the traditional gesture. She took a deep breath and stooped. His warm, gentle hands clasped her upper arms and drew her up. her. She smiled at him. He embraced her, put a sweetmeat into her mouth and gave her a box. She opened it and took out gold earrings and a nose ring set with diamonds. He smiled at her. "Happy New Year, Indira. May Srimati Sita, the Goddess of fortune bless you."

"Thank you for my beautiful present. Have a very, very, happy New Year," she mumbled through the mouthful of burfi.

Grateful for the suggestion, she looked at her kind, helpful brother who, as her parents often said, was an ideal son, brother, grandson, and nephew. More important to the family than her because he was the son who would inherit the business, and, when she married, she would be part of another family, she loved him so much that she was never jealous. "Thanks for the very good advice."

* * *

In her bedroom, after she and Gopal had been blessed by Kaka and Kaki, Indira made the beds while she waited for her friend to come out of the shower.

"Why did your family touch each other's feet?" Daisy asked, her voice sharp as the edge of a razor blade, when she entered the room wrapped in a towel.

"It's a custom."

Daisy discarded the towel and put on her underwear. "Well!" She sniffed. "I wouldn't bow down to anyone!"

"What are you going to wear today?" Indira asked, hoping to distract her friend.

"A denim jacket and jeans and a white blouse."

"Unless you want to borrow a sari from me."

Daisy shook her head. "No, thank you."

Indira shrugged. "Okay. We'll have breakfast when you are ready."

"Aren't you going to explain?"

"What?" Indira asked to give herself time to think of what to say.

"You know."

"Oh, that," Indira said as nonchalantly as possible. "It's a tradition. On New Year's

Day we wear new clothes and touch our elder's feet out of respect. In return, we receive their blessings and gifts."

"It shocked me."

Indira shrugged. No less than we were when we saw Daisy watching us wearing those thin pajamas.

"Don't make a mountain out of a molehill. It's only our tradition."

Daisy scowled. "I think it's humiliating."

"Only because we have different customs. What about your one of even kissing strange men under the mistletoe? I can't imagine allowing any man other than my future husband to kiss me."

"But-" Daisy began.

"I'm hungry we can eat breakfast at the breakfast bar," Indira said, pleased with an excuse to escape from her friend.

Things have changed, Indira thought sadly as she went slowly downstairs, Yesterday, I'm sure Daisy would have jumped at the chance to wear one of my saris.

* * *

"Let's go and see Srimati Radha and Sri Krishna before we have breakfast," Indira suggested.

"What does Sri and, what-did-you-say, mean?"

"Sri means lord and Srimati means lady."

Really, though we've been friends for so long, I didn't understand how religious Indira is. Strange ways she and her family have, even if there's nothing wrong with them. The Nathwanis might think my belief in the Holy Trinity strange. She peeped through her eyelashes at Indira.

"Why do you want to see them?"

Indira led her downstairs and opened the temple room door before she spoke. "To present myself to them and ask for something."

Indira's grandfather, who sat on the floor in front of the altar, looked up from his book. "Sometimes our prayers are answered not in the way we anticipate."

"But Dada, you've always told me to pray to Krishna and Radharani."

Daisy gazed at the dignified old man. "What do you ask for, sir?"

"To forgive my mistakes and serve them perfectly."

"Oh!"

"I understand you are puzzled. Please allow me to explain. We must serve something or someone even if we only serve ourselves. For example, parents serve their children by looking after them. So, tell me if there is anyone better than God to serve?"

Daisy shrugged and toyed with the ends of her loose hair. She looked at Indira, who stood before the altar, the palms of her hands pressed together in prayer.

Daisy breathed in the scent of incense which she identified as sandalwood, and admired Krishna and Radha's new clothes and flower garlands made with dahlias.

"What did you pray for," she asked when Indira's hands parted. "Do you believe that if you tell anyone you won't get what you asked for?"

"No. I prayed to be allowed to stay with you at Christmas. Please come with me to have breakfast. I expect Ba and Kaki are waiting for me to finish mine and then to help to prepare a New Year feast."

Indira's dad came out of the lounge into the hall.

"Good morning, Princess. Good morning, Daisy, have you had breakfast?"

"Not yet." Daisy's tummy rumbled.

Bapuji smiled at them. "Eat now because we're going to be busy all day."

"Busy?" Daisy asked.

"Yes," he said. "We will welcome our relations, friends and business associates who will come to give us sweets and other treats and we will reciprocate at their houses."

"Oh, that sounds like fun," Daisy said.

"Yes, it will be," Indira agreed, and led her into the kitchen.

"Good morning, Mrs Nathwani, good Morning, Mrs N.," Daisy said. "I'm sorry for coming downstairs in my pajamas.

"You're forgiven," Ba said.

Kaki frowned "Provided you never make that mistake again."

"I promise I won't," she said, delighted because she might be invited to stay with them again.

"May we have breakfast, before Daisy's mum comes to take her home?" Indira asked.

Daisy crossed her fingers behind her back, hoping Indira would be allowed to spend Christmas at her home.

Chapter Four

"Help yourselves to breakfast, girls," Mrs Nathwani said while she and Mrs N put sweets and small portions of savoury snacks on stainless steel plates with deep rims.

"I shall give one to your mother, Daisy. I hope both of you will enjoy the treats," Mrs N. said.

Daisy's mouth watered. "Thank you, Mrs N, I'm sure we will."

Indira asked, "Daisy, do you want cornflakes, toast and marmalade and a cup of tea for breakfast?"

"Yes, please," Daisy said, relieved because, much as she enjoyed spicy food at other times, she didn't fancy it for breakfast.

"Sit down at the breakfast bar while I fetch everything." Indira said. "Do you want chunky marmalade or shredded marmalade?"

"Chunky please." Daisy pulled out two stools and looked around as she sat at the breakfast bar. Her mum, a keen cook, would love to have a large kitchen like this, which was four times the size of theirs.

She had nearly finished eating her breakfast when Mr Nathwani led her mum into the kitchen.

"Would you like something to eat, Julia?" he asked.

"No thank you, I've already eaten."

"A cup of tea?" Mrs Nathwani asked.

"No, thank you, Kumud."

"All right," Indira's father said. "We won't try to persuade you to change your mind. If you'll excuse me, ladies, I'll leave you to chat."

Mum looked at him. "Can you spare a moment? Before Daisy and I go shopping, to tell me if the girls have sorted out their arrangements for Christmas?"

"I beg your pardon. Did you say their arrangements?"

Indira's eyes pleaded with him while she waited for his reply.

"You're chewing the lip again, Indira. One day, when you're in a state, you'll draw blood," Daisy whispered.

"Govinda, it would be a pleasure to have Indira with us at Christmas," Mum said.

His forehead creased. "It is kind of you to invite Indira, but she must stay here."

"Why can't she share it with us? Kumud, please ask your husband to change his mind. You and your family have done so much for us. You collect the girls from school more often than I do and Daisy visits your house more frequently than Indira comes to mine."

Mrs Nathwani glanced at her husband.

"Please change your mind, Bapuji?"

"No, Indira." He sounded annoyed. "Your mother and I prefer you to remain at home. Don't argue." He looked at Mum. "Julia, thank you for your kind invitation. I hope you're not offended by my refusal," he said, then added. "Daisy, I look forward to seeing you again."

Mum frowned. "Why does Indira rarely go anywhere without one of her family? It even seems you're always reluctant to allow her to come to our house. I hope you won't be put out by my saying you should let her have some independence. You can't baby her forever."

The expression in Mr Nathwani's eyes hardened like a pair of icicles. "Indira can rely on us to protect her."

"From what?" Mum asked, obviously astonished.

"Anything which might distress her or ruin her future," he said, obviously irritated.

Mum opened her mouth to say something. He forestalled her. "Forgive me for not having time to say more. Before our guests arrive, we have a lot to do." He strode to the door and left the kitchen.

Poor Indira. Daisy looked at her friend, whose forehead creased into a deep frown, her cheeks flaming and tears spilling from her eyes. "Your dad might change his mind," she said to calm her but did not believe he would.

"You're always optimistic, Daisy, but I don't think my husband will." Mrs Nathwani gazed at Mum. "Julia, Christmas day is a public holiday when our business closes for two days. I'm sure you can appreciate my husband wants Indira and Gopal to spend it with us."

Daisy sighed. A mere excuse.

Mrs N cleared her throat. "Julia are you sure you don't want a cup of tea before you leave?"

"I'd like to, but I can't spare the time. We have a lot to do. Have you packed your bag, Daisy?"

Daisy ate the last morsel of toast and gulped the rest of her tea. "Yes, Mum, it's in the hall."

Mrs Nathwani covered a plate with a serviette, picked it up, and offered it to Mum. "This is for you and Daisy. On New Year's Day it's our custom to give one to all our friends. I hope you will enjoy the treats."

"That's kind of you. I shall reciprocate at Christmas with vegetarian ones." Mum's smile did not warm her eyes. "Thank you for inviting Daisy to celebrate Diwali with you and your family. I'm sure she enjoyed it. Come along, Daisy. We must stock up for the week and buy shoes for you. It's really time for us to leave."

"Mrs Nathwani, thanks ever so much for having me. Indira, I'll see you at school tomorrow."

"Ba, may Daisy come to tea tomorrow? We could do our homework together."

"Yes, if Julia doesn't mind, I'll collect you and your friend from school and bring both of you to our house."

"Do you mind, Mrs. Royston?" Indira asked.

"Bless you, I don't. I know how much you girls enjoy being together." Mum looked at Indira's mother. "If you agree, Indira may come to my house on Saturday."

Mrs Nathwani smiled. "I hope Daisy will enjoy it."

"That's settled," Mum said. "We'll say goodbye for now."

* * *

"Daisy, the weather's mild for this time of the year and the sun's shining," Mum said as soon as they left the house. "I fancy a walk to stretch my legs before we go shopping. Shall we go for a short one across The Green and leave my car parked up the road?"

"Don't your feet ache?"

"I took the day off, so they're okay."

Poor Mum managed a greeting card shop and spent most of her working hours on her feet, but often managed a break to collect her from school. Daisy wished she didn't have to work so hard. When she was older, she wanted to get a Saturday job to help her.

They walked towards the large pond, her favourite place in a tranquil area. Mum might appreciate a rest because, although she never complained, her feet were often sore. Daisy pointed at one of the nearby wooden benches paid for by relatives of a deceased person. Daisy always read the brief inscription and name on a brass plaque attached to a bench. Did the person go to heaven or hell as Christians believed or did the soul take birth in another body as Indira believed. "Shall we sit?"

"A penny for your thoughts," Mum said.

"They aren't worth it. Shall we sit?"

"Yes. This is my favourite place in the park."

They sat next to each other and laughed at the ducks that hurried toward them and quacked, demanding food. "Sorry," Mum said, "Nothing for you today." She glanced at the woods on the perimeter stretching a quarter of a mile or less to a housing estate. "If you ever walk home alone after dark, take the well-lit road, not the shortcut through here to town. I don't want you to be in The Green when there might be dangerous hooligans up to no good. You're a very sensible girl. I know I can trust you not to risk running into trouble."

"Don't worry, Mum, when you can't collect me from the Nathwani's house one of them always gives me a lift."

The sun hid behind a bank of dark clouds. Daisy shivered, as though they foretold something dreadful was imminent. Occasionally, she experienced inexplicable premonitions she could not decipher that often came true. Drops of rain splattered onto her. "Let's go before it pours."

Mum unfurled her umbrella. "Don't worry, I'm not made of sugar." She pointed in the direction of their home. "Not for love or money would you catch Indira's mum or aunt walking across The Green and sitting here." She sniffed. "Some people think they're a cut above everyone else."

"Do your really believe they are?"

Mum laughed. "No, I'm only a bit put out with them because I know how much you wanted Indira to share Christmas with us." The rain drops increased and cascaded onto them. Mum linked her free arm with her. "There's room for both of us under the umbrella."

"Everything smells good after a downpour. Indira's grandfather told me that in the scripture, the Bhagavad Gita, it's reported Krishna stated, 'I am the fragrance of the earth after the rain.'"

"Oh, well, that's a nice description, but don't get carried away by the Nathwani's beliefs and religion."

"I won't."

"Did you have a nice time during Diwali, darling?"

"Yes, I did, but I'm still disappointed because Indira can't come to us for Christmas."

Her mother hunched her shoulders.

"By the way, Mum, I wish you hadn't said that one day the Nathwanis must stop babying Indira."

"I speak as I find."

Daisy laughed. "You sound like Gran did," she said, because Mum had used one of the old lady's favourite phrases.

"Do I?" Her mother smiled.

"Yes, you do."

"Thank you for the compliment."

* * *

On the following day, Daisy enjoyed a substantial tea at the Nathwanis house before Mum picked her up at seven o'clock. When they reached home, Mum opened the garden gate and Daisy followed her along the garden path and up the steps to the porch. Mum hunted for her keys in her handbag and opened the door. Inside the porch, her mother furled her umbrella and stood it in a tall red vase. They took off their coats and hung them on the stand, then put their gloves and scarves in a drawer beneath it. Mum always insisted everything should be clean and tidy.

Her mother inserted the key into the lock of the pillar-box-red front door, which had a semi-circular stained-glass window inserted into the top. Electric light from the glass enclosed porch with a white wood frame shone through it, casting green, red, and yellow patterns onto the hall floor.

"Home sweet home," Mum said, as she stepped indoors.

Daisy sighed happily. Much smaller and not as luxurious as the Nathwani's house, her thrifty Mum had created a beautiful, comfortable home on the proverbial shoestring. She appreciated the yellow wallpaper and cream paint, the slightly faded second-hand oriental rug, and a large copper jug filled with dried flowers and grasses on a mahogany whatnot. Looking at the hall, no-one would guess Mum scoured car boot sales, flea markets, jumble sales and charity shops for bargains. On the walls on each side of the stairs hung pictures of rural scenes. Mum hadn't paid more than a pound for any of them. Put together, they made an attractive display.

Daisy exclaimed. "Mum!"

"What?"

"Indira's really upset because she can't spend Christmas with us."

"There's nothing we can do about it, love."

"I wish she could come."

"Don't fret, instead put the kettle on for a cuppa."

"What's up, Mum?" Daisy asked in tune with every inflexion of her mother's voice.

"Nothing's wrong. I was deciding whether to cook a chicken instead of a turkey for lunch on Christmas Day. I don't want to eat leftovers from a large bird for days."

Daisy winced at the idea of eating a dead bird.

"Don't pull faces. You talked me into allowing you to become a vegetarian and persuaded me to give up red meat, but I'll not be done out of my Christmas lunch and with all the trimmings, including sage and onion stuffing."

"Chickens and turkeys suffer as much as animals when they are slaughtered," Daisy said.

"I daresay, but it's over in a minute so I don't want to hear more about it."

"If the trimmings are cooked with the dead bird, I don't want to eat any."

"Oh, don't be so pernickety, Daisy. I'll make yours separately. Smile. I'm sure we'll enjoy Christmas. And who knows? Anything might happen. The Nathwanis might allow Indira to spend it with us."

* * *

On Saturday afternoon at Daisy's house, she and Indira sat next to each other on a comfortable sofa opposite the television and leafed through magazines for teenagers.

Daisy handed Indira one. "Read this."

"What?"

Daisy rolled her eyes theatrically. "The article about two sisters sent to Pakistan on the pretext of a holiday. Their parents planned to force them to marry men they would not meet until their wedding days.

Fortunately, one of the unlucky girls contacted the British Embassy in time to be rescued and brought back to England. Would your parents play a trick like that on you?"

Indira shook her head. "You've been coming to our house for long enough to know better than that. Anyway, although I know ignorant no-hopers call me Paki, I tell them I'm neither from Pakistan nor a Muslim. My parents love me. They wouldn't trick me into going to India to marry a man I'd never met."

Daisy yawned. "I don't know if I'll ever want to have a husband." She sipped Coca-Cola, then added. "We should write for magazines. How much do you think they'd pay?"

"What would you write?"

"I'd write about mum and dad. They never got married because they didn't believe a piece of paper is necessary to prove couples love each other."

Indira pushed the magazine aside and asked. "How do you feel about that?"

"The only thing which bothers me is that Dad died when I was two years old. Mum says he loved me to bits, but I can't remember him."

"You never speak about his family."

Daisy sighed. "There's not much to say. Dad was American. Mum has only told me his relations didn't approve of, as they put it, them not marrying in church and dad living in sin with Mum." She blinked. "I don't want to talk about them."

"But your mum Is called Mrs Royston not Miss Royston."

Daisy shifted on the sofa. "Yes, well, Gran thought it would be better for me."

They nibbled popcorn, drank Coca-Cola, and read the magazines, until Indira spoke.

"They had a huge, traditional, Hindu wedding in a temple followed by one in a registry office to make it legal."

"Do you want a wedding like that?"

"My parents will expect me to, but not until I'm at least eighteen years old, or after I go to college or university. Times are changing. Ba was sixteen and Bapuji was twenty and they were chaperoned when they met a few times. Dadi married Dada, who she did not meet until her wedding day when she was thirteen, and my father was born a year later."

"That's shocking." Daisy opened another packet of crisps and offered it to Indira. "Your grandmother was a year younger than us when your grandfather was born. I think it's very unusual for such a young girl in England to have a baby." She flipped open the magazine she was reading. "But there's an article about an English girl who had the first of her three kids when she was fifteen."

Indira raised her eyebrows. "Really?"

"Yes, read it yourself, if you want to."

"In India girls may be married when they are very young," Indira said.

"And they may in America. I read about mountain girls getting married when they're only ten or eleven years old." Daisy's mind wandered while they munched crisps. "I wonder who I'll fall in love with. One thing's for sure, I'm not going to - you know - copy some girls at school and do it with someone I don't love to find out what it's like. I'll wait till I'm in love, really in love."

"You'd prefer a partner to a husband?"

"I don't know. I'd need to trust him not to - how did my gran put it? – love me and leave me if he didn't marry me. Anyway, I'd talk it over with Mum. What would you do?"

"I could never shame my family."

"Shame?"

"My community's attitude to love and marriage is different to yours. If I returned late or stayed out all night, my family would suspect I'd been with a boy. I would be booted out of the house. Parents wouldn't consider any other reason for a respectable girl not to come home without telling her parents where she had been without their consent. As for having a partner instead of a husband, they would cut me out of their lives. The question of my being so badly brought up that I would even chat to boys I am not related to doesn't arise. It would be shameful to let them down. Ba and Bapuji trust me, and I respect them. As for Dada, admiration, love, and respect means I could never disgrace him."

Daisy wrinkled her forehead. "Would you agree to an arranged marriage?"

"Today, that's not as bad as English people imagine. My parents want me to be happy. They will introduce me to a prospective husband from a respectable family in which I would be treated well. After meeting several times and given the opportunity to speak to each other without being overheard, we could decide if we want to marry." Indira shrugged. "None of us know what the future holds, but, thankfully, I do know my life will be different to my great-great grandmother's. She was eleven when she wed, thirteen when her son was born, and fourteen when she became a sati."

"What is that?" Daisy asked.

"A sati is a widow who burns herself on her husband's funeral pyre." Indira took the video of the Ramayana out of her brightly embroidered, homespun cloth bag.

"Oh my God! That doesn't bear thinking about," Daisy exclaimed.

"No, it doesn't. Even though sati became illegal, if a determined woman wanted to commit it, or the family insisted, the custom continued."

"But your great-great grandma was a child, not a woman." Daisy pushed aside the packet of crisps. "I feel sick."

"Oh no. I shouldn't have told you. I know how squeamish you are."

Daisy gasped. "Indira, surely no woman would agree burn herself to death."

"I think a voluntary sati believes she will share the karma for her husband's good deeds."

"That sounds risky. She might suffer for his bad ones. But what happened to a sati's children?"

"Most widows with young children weren't allowed to become sati's. But my great-great grandfather had two wives. Before my great-grandmother, his first wife, sat next to him on the funeral pyre, she asked his second wife to bring up her son."

"Gross!" exclaimed Daisy.

"No more than what's going on in this country. So many people get drunk, take drugs, and commit suicide. And this is supposed to be a civilised society. Still, it's their choice."

Daisy shuddered and put a cushion behind her head. "That's true, but I can't bear to talk about sati anymore."

"Shall we watch the video?"

Daisy nodded.

"I'll refill your glass with Coca-Cola?"

Daisy shook her head. "No, don't, I still feel sick."

Indira slotted in the video and pressed play. "There are English sub-titles but ask me if you have any questions."

Chapter Five

Daisy sighed with pleasure at the end of the epic about Rama and his consort, Sita, who was abducted by the demon, Ravana, and rescued by an army of monkey warriors led by Hanuman. Enthralled by the settings, the gorgeous clothes, and the contrast between noble and ignoble characters, she enjoyed it so much that she decided to buy a copy with her precious pocket money.

She stood. "Mum's tired when she comes home so she expects the house will be a tidy house. She'll be here soon. Would you mind helping me, Indira?

"Of course not."

"Shall we clean the kitchen?"

"Yes."

They took their dirty glasses, empty bottles, and bowls to the untidy kitchen.

"Oh!" Indira pointed at the eggcup with an eggshell in it, and an empty tin of salmon Mum had left on a counter. "Daisy, I don't mind helping you, but I can't help you in here. What can I do?"

She should have remembered her friend was too strict a vegetarian to touch anything used for meat, fish, or eggs.

"Okay, I'll do it after I've tidied the sitting room."

"I'll help you do that." Indira followed her. "When the housework's done we should get on with our homework before your mum comes home?"

"If it's all right with you, I'll do mine tomorrow," Daisy said.

"Okay, but I must finish mine today. Tomorrow I'm going to my cousin, Sunita's wedding at Bhaktivedanta Manor which George Harrison bought for the Hare Krishna devotees to convert into a temple."

"But he's a famous pop singer. Why did he do that?"

Indira shrugged. "I suppose he likes them. Anyway, I'm looking forward to the wedding."

"Was your cousin's marriage arranged by the family?"

"In a manner of speaking. Her parents know the bridegroom's family is respectable and asked a relative to suggest Sunita meet him. The couple's horoscopes were in tune, so her parents invited his family to a meal. Their son, Proful, and Sunita liked what they saw of each other. They were given the opportunity to chat to each other without being overheard. When he asked her to marry him, she accepted him." Indira sighed. "It's romantic. They are in love and I'm sure they'll be happy."

"With their families all but breathing over their shoulders it doesn't sound like a romance, but I hope you will enjoy the wedding."

"I shall. Then it's back to school."

Daisy frowned. "I'm sick of school and tired of homework. I'll be glad when it's the Christmas holidays."

"At least your mum isn't always on your case."

Daisy raised her eyebrows. "What do you mean? You're so clever that you don't need to work hard."

"You're wrong. If I'm not in the top three, my parents will send me to a tutor during the holidays."

"Why? If they plan an arranged marriage for you after you leave school what do your results matter?"

"I've already explained they are not too old-fashioned to allow me to go to college or university, provided I live at home."

"Yes, of course. Sorry. Blimey, I must crack on. It's five o'clock. Mum will be here in an hour, and I haven't made the beds." She smiled at Indira. "Anyway, we wouldn't have time to do homework before she gets here."

"Do you mind doing chores?"

"Sometimes, but Mum works very hard to put food on the table. I love her and want to do whatever I can to help her."

Indira returned the round, glass-topped coffee table to the middle of the room and stacked the magazines on to shelf beneath the top of it. "The sitting room's tidy. Shall I make the beds and tidy them while you get on in the kitchen?"

"Yes, please."

* * *

In Mrs Royston's bedroom, decorated in shades of yellow and cream, Indira straightened the sheets and blankets, plumped up the lace-edged pillows, and put them in place. She covered the bed with a quilted bedspread the colour of old gold and drew the curtains.

Indira looked around. Before Dada won the lottery, they were crammed together in a shabby house only a little larger than this, which the family didn't know could be improved with cheap, second-hand items. Mrs Royston made the best of this one. She had something money couldn't buy – good taste. Her house is as comfortable and nice as our one, although my family spend thousands of pounds and Mrs Royston only has a tiny fraction of that amount to spend.

The front door opened. "I'm home," Mrs Royston called.

"Hi, Mum, I'm in the kitchen.

Wondering if good-natured Mrs. Royston would be cross because Daisy let her tidy the bedroom, Indira rushed out onto the narrow landing.

"Shall I put the kettle on for a cuppa, Mum?"

"Yes, please, darling. What a good, kind girl you are."

Indira hurried downstairs to the hall.

"Hello, sweetie, have you and Daisy had a good time?" Mrs Royston asked as they entered the kitchen.

"Yes, thank you."

"We really did, Mum."

"What did you do?" Mrs Royston sank down onto the high kitchen stool.

"We watched the legend about Rama and Sita set in India in ancient times."

"Not a legend, history," Indira said and didn't understand why Daisy's mum frowned at her.

"Oh! Whatever it is, I'm glad you enjoyed it, Daisy," Mrs Royston said.

"I did. When it ended, time was running out for me. While I cleaned the kitchen, Indira cleaned upstairs and made your bed."

"I hope you don't mind me making your bed I mean," Indira said obviously too anxious to consider her grammar.

"Of course, I don't mind, but you mustn't let this daughter of mine turn you into a slave. How are you?"

"Fine, thank you, Mrs Royston. I hope you are well."

"I am, thank you. What else have the two of you been doing today?"

Worried, Indira looked at the plate of biscuits Daisy put on the table. Would she tell her mother she and her friend nearly had a quarrel about sati, something she would never come to terms with? If she did, what would Mrs Royston say?

"Nothing much, Mum. We chatted, watched the film, and did the housework. Indira was about to do her homework when you came home."

Daisy hurried to find out who rang the doorbell and saw Mr Nathwani standing outside.

"Hello, Daisy, I'm here to take Indira home."

"Hello, please come in." Daisy shut the door, then looked back into the kitchen. "Indira, your father's here," she called.

Daisy's mother entered the hall. "Good evening, Mr Nathwani."

"Good evening."

"A cup of tea? Something to eat?" she asked.

He smiled and shook his head. "No thank you, Julia. I've had a very busy day. We're always rushed off our feet at work when Christmas draws near. I need to go home and have an early night after dinner."

Indira waited for Daisy and her mum to leave before she spoke. "Bapuji, I wish I could help you and Kaka in the office."

"When you're older, maybe we'll allow you to. For now, Princess, concentrate on doing well at school."

"I shall." Indira sighed and looked away from him. "I'll fetch my schoolbag." She brought it from the lounge. "Bapuji, may Daisy come to us next Saturday?"

"Yes, if your Ba doesn't have any plans and Julia doesn't mind."

"It's fine by me," said Mrs Royston.

Bapuji opened the front door and held it open. "Come along, Indira."

"Goodbye Daisy. See you at school. Thank you for having me, Mrs Royston."

"It's always a pleasure, sweetie."

"Bye Indira," Daisy said.

* * *

"What did you and Daisy do today?" Bapuji asked as they walked down the garden path to his car parked by the side of the road.

"We watched the Ramayana."

Bapujj opened the passenger door of his metallic gold Lexus, waited for her to sit, and closed it. He sat next to her in front and turned the key in the ignition. The engine purred. "What did Daisy think of the film?"

"She liked it. Seeing Srimati Sita touch Sri Rama's feet, might have helped her to understand that our customs are...are-"

"Rooted in the past. When your kaka and I were children, we touched our parents' feet every morning and received their blessings."

"Every morning! I thought that only happens in Indian movies."

He chuckled. "It didn't do us any harm. It reminded us to respect our elders and not question their judgement. We don't expect you and Gopal to follow the custom because we know you respect your elders, don't need to prove it, and are sure neither of you will ever disappoint us." The car surged forward. "You can't imagine how much we appreciated our parents. In India, they dealt in cotton and lost a fortune when their warehouses on the banks of the Ganges were burnt during the struggle for independence. Your dadi's older brother had settled in Uganda where he prospered. He suggested your great-grandfather and grandmother should make a fresh start. By the time they were forced out of the country, our family was rich." He sighed. "I'll say no more because you know how difficult it was for our family to settle here. By Sri Krishna's mercy our family worked extremely hard and prospered. You will have a large dowry and Gopal will inherit our successful business."

The gate to the drive on the left of their front garden stood open. Bapuji drove the car to the garage. He glanced at her and sighed. "Do you and Gopal realise how lucky you are? You're the first members of our family to have the chance of getting a degree."

"Do you wish you went to university?" she asked as she got out of the car.

"You ask too many questions. Princess, go indoors, it's too cold to stand here talking."

"Bapuji-"

He laughed. "A degree wouldn't have done me any harm, but I would not have helped your Dada to establish our successful import export venture. I'm content as I am."

* * *

Half-awake on Sunday morning, Indira's mind was filled with jumbled thoughts. Now that she and Daisy were nearly fifteen, they were not always in harmony. She scowled. Kaka and Kaki disapproved of her friendship with Daisy since her friend entered the temple room dressed in pajamas. Ba and Bapuji had merely commented that after so many years during which Daisy visited their house she should have known better.

The bed covers over her face, she lay still, reviewing their recent conversations and again envying her friend's freedom. If Daisy fell in and out of love half a dozen times before she settled down with a partner or husband, her mum wouldn't think badly of her. Fortunate Daisy, if the relationship didn't work out, her mum wouldn't shun her. Her own family was too strict. They should trust her not to shame them, but they would never tolerate her sharing so much as a drink in a coffee bar with a male friend, surrounded by other people. If she chose a husband who they did not introduce her to, they would be furious and if she defied them and married him, she would be cast out of the family. If she agreed to an arranged marriage then complained she was unhappy, they would be sorry but tell her to try harder to please her husband and in-laws. Although a few brave ladies divorced their husbands if she did it would be unacceptable to all her relatives and their community.

She couldn't breathe in the warm, claustrophobic stuffiness under the bedcovers. She pushed them off her face and peered into the gloom caused by drawn curtains that banished daylight. She opened her eyes, looked at the clock's luminous dial. Oh no, I'm late for school. Indira pushed back the bedcovers, stood, and laughed. Silly me! It's Sunday. Instead of having a shower, and dressing before going downstairs to the temple room for morning service, then helping Ba and Kaki cook breakfast for the family, she snuggled down again, ignoring the guilt not strong enough to make her get up. Perhaps she would not be scolded for being lazy because she came first or second in class in every subject except biology, which she loathed after being expected to dissect a poor little dead frog. She pressed the palms of her hands together. Thank you, Sri Krishna, I'm sure You helped me to get good marks, so I don't need tuition. She sighed with relief. Her overworked brain could rest.

Ba opened the bedroom door and clicked on the light switch. "Jai Shri Krishna," she murmured the familiar greeting that wished Lord Krishna victory.

"Jai Sri Krishna," Indira responded.

"You're already awake. Why didn't you get up?" Ba's voice sharpened with concern. "Are you sick? Have you got a fever?"

Before she could answer Ba touched her forehead.

Indira turned her head aside. "Don't worry Ba, I'm fine."

"Good, it's more than time for you to get up, there's a lot to do. After breakfast we'll make enough lemon pickle to last for months." Ba frowned. "Take that sulky expression off your face."

* * *

Resentful after breakfast, Indira plucked up her courage to protest and voice her opinion. "Ba, our family imports pickles, and chutneys from India. I don't understand why you and Kaki make them instead of ordering them from the warehouse."

"We prefer to make them for Sri Krishna. I always hope He will relish them and ask for more when your Dada serves them to Him and, if you're honest, Indira, you'll agree home-made is best."

"I don't agree, some of the readymade ones are as good."

Ba's eyes glinted. "They don't taste as nice to me."

"Daisy's mum bought -"

"Julia doesn't know how to make our Indian pickles but -"

"Ba!"

"I was about to say although she makes delicious jam. Gopal really liked the blackberry and apple one she gave us." Ba tightened the lid on the last jar. "Next time you'll be able to make lemon pickle without my help."

"Indira, you're learning to cook for your own good. When you marry your in-laws will expect you to be an expert cook," Kaki chipped in.

The cold expressions in her mother and aunt's eyes warned her not to say more.

"Ba, I'm hungry and thirsty. May I have Coca-Cola and crisps?"

Ba fetched the large, stainless-steel container of homemade ones and put it on the breakfast bar. "Sit down, Indira." She fetched a plate, serving spoon, a glass, then served her.

"Aren't you hungry, Ba? Don't you want something to eat or drink?"

Ba shook her head. Her long gold earrings swayed and cast shadows on her smooth, unblemished cheeks. A loose curl from her hair, coiled into a bun low on the back of her head, fell lightly to her shoulder.

Although her beautiful mother gave birth to her and her brother, she could still star in a film. Ba had won prizes at school and was intelligent enough to have a career. Was she happy being a housewife and mother? Would she like to have more than she had? Even if Ba had problems or was discontented, she would never admit it, no matter how much she questioned her. Her mother believed she must always be cheerful. Well, Ba had something in common with Daisy's grandmother, who had often said. 'It's no use grumbling, what can't be cured must be endured," then added. 'Weep and you weep alone. Laugh and the world laughs with you."

"What are you thinking about, Indira?" Ba asked.

"Nothing in particular." She glanced at her mother. "You work too hard and must be tired. Sit down and take the weight off your feet."

"No, Gopal will soon come home to have lunch. I've time to make one of his favourite curries, aubergines with a spiced filling, which your dada will offer to Sri Krishna with His lunch."

Indira sipped Coca-Cola.

"Do you want to dip crisps into the tomato chutney I made yesterday?" Kaki asked.

"No thank you," Indira said, tired of being fussed over and treated like a child. If she wanted some, she could have served herself. Suddenly, her mother and aunt's loving watchfulness became unbearable.

"Are you sure," Kaki persisted.

"Yes, I don't like chutney with them," she fibbed.

Chapter Six

Indira left the kitchen, showered, and dressed in a mauve sari with a green and purple pattern woven into it. Downstairs she entered the temple room, inhaled fragrant incense offered to Radha and Krishna, and rang the brass bell suspended from the ceiling to announce her arrival.

Dada, dressed in spotless white, gold-rimmed glasses perched on the bridge of his nose stopped reciting verses from the Bhagavadgita devotees believed Krishna spoke. He looked at her. "Did you help your mother to make pickles?"

"Yes," Indira replied, her tone sharper than she intended. She tried not to reveal her irritation as she fetched a cloth, and a wicker basket containing crimson and white roses imported from overseas, a ball of white crochet cotton, a needle, and scissors. She sat down on a cushion, opposite her grandfather, spread a clean white cloth on the floor in front of her and put the roses on it.

"By the time you get married, you will be an expert cook like your late grandmother, mother and aunt," Dada said gently.

"I never want to be treated like a servant and spend hours and hours making pickles instead of buying them."

"In this house all of us are servants of Srimati Radharani and Sri Krishna. And that, my child, includes making pickles for them." He smiled. "When I was a child, my mother's pickles always tasted best. I can almost smell them. She made many varieties with love and devotion to offer to Lord Krishna, hoping He would relish whatever she made before we ate after them. You should be glad your mother and aunt are teaching you to make pickles to be offered to our deities."

She appreciated Dada's attempt to help her come to terms with the demands made on her time, but she was not glad.

Indira arranged the fragrant roses in patterns on the cloth to make garlands for Sri Krishna and Srimati Radharani. Their colour would complement the crimson silk clothes they would wear tomorrow. She threaded the needle and pushed it through the first flower. "Dada, don't you agree that these days there's more for a modern girl than cooking? Many things have changed. For example, nowadays few widows commit sati, something Daisy can't get her head around." And to be honest with herself, neither could she.

"Explain to Daisy that according to our scriptures, thousands of years ago, only a woman who wanted to committed sati. By the time the British ruled India, the custom was already corrupt and countless women were forced to burn on their husbands' funeral pyres until the British government outlawed it. Today, the ritual self-sacrifice is not prevalent, but some widows insist on observing it despite the Indian Government's law that it is illegal."

Her hands stilled. "If Daisy asks more questions, no matter how I try to justify sati, I'm sure she won't understand."

"Say that she doesn't understand the custom, and we don't understand Holy Communion when Christians drink wine and eat bread which represent Lord Jesus' blood and flesh. Perhaps the rite once brought Christians close to their beloved Lord, but it became less meaningful over the centuries to some people. For example, Daisy's grandmother was a devout servant of Jesus Christ who took Holy Communion every Sunday, but Daisy and her mother don't. Explain to Daisy that although we believe Sri Krishna is the supreme form of God, she should not have a have a quarrel with other faiths whose followers worship our God in separate ways."

Indira giggled.

Dada stared at her and raised his eyebrows.

"I'm sorry. I laughed because I remembered I was ten years old when Bapuji was ill in bed, and we were alone in the house. A man, who said he was his friend, came, and asked to see him. I took him to Bapuji's bedroom. It turned out that he was a Jehovah's witness. When Bapuji asked him to leave, he refused and continued preaching. Bapuji had to wait for Ba to come home to get rid of the man. When Bapuji scolded me, I understood the stranger entered the house under false pretenses, and that I should never admit someone I didn't know. Anyway, I didn't think much of his beliefs."

Her grandfather's lips twitched, but he didn't say anything.

"Everything you say makes sense, Dada. I shall never forget it," she said, hastily, realising that sometimes, to preserve their friendship, she and Daisy must agree to disagree and respect each other's beliefs.

While she made the garlands, and Dada made a red and gold silk turban for Krishna to wear tomorrow, her thoughts flickered here, there, and everywhere. She glanced at him. Suddenly, she realised how little she knew about him. What was it really like for him when her great-grandparents became bankrupts?

During Mahatma Gandhi's struggle for Independence, when he inspired the nation to spin their own cotton instead of wearing imports, her family was ruined. The market for the imported material, made from cotton grown in India, spun in England, and exported to India that filled their warehouses disappeared. Chandra, her great-grandfather received an invitation to live with great-grandmother's younger brother, who had settled in Uganda, an underdeveloped British protectorate.

"Dada what was it like when he and your parents went to Uganda?"

"Humiliation for my father. A nightmare for my mother, whose family and my father's family were very wealthy merchants, who had employed many servants. In Kampala there was a time when my mother had to look after her brother's children, cook, clean, wash clothes and iron. Worst of all, she was forced to tolerate her sister-in-law's spite. That woman wanted to get her out of the house."

"Why?"

"My aunt was jealous because my uncle loved your Dadi so much. She hid some money under my mother's pillow to turn him against her."

Indignant, Indira sympathised with her Dadi. "I know the story, Dada."

"It's not a story, it's family history. When my uncle came home from work, my aunt wept and told him her money had been stolen. He gave an order for the house to be searched. Well, although the money was found under my mother's mattress, my father never doubted her innocence."

Indira threaded her needle and began to make the second garland.

"Penniless, Father and Mother left the house and lived under a jacaranda tree at the end of the street." Aware that Dada was very proud of them, Indira's hands sat still, the garland neglected on the cloth. "People came from miles around to see relatives of a rich man living so humbly and help them. My poor mother covered her head with the end of her sari, too shy to look at men to whom she was not related. Of course, Uncle couldn't bear the shame of his relations living like beggars and attracting so much interest. He pleaded with them to return and promised his wife would apologise, behave herself in the future, and not treat Mother like a servant."

"What did Great-grandfather do?"

"He lived under the tree, worshipped his deities and prayed for protection."

"And Sri Krishna provided for him?"

"Yes. Relatives in India sent bales of cotton cloth, which had not been destroyed, to my father. He sold them and ploughed the profit into more imported goods. His investments yielded excellent returns. He prospered, until he and my mother left their bodies, before British subjects, including, as you know, our family were expelled from Uganda." He smiled and put the turbans in an ornately carved cedarwood box.

"We prospered after I won the lottery."

"So, Dada, all's well that ends well, but I suppose you still disapprove of me for wanting to buy pickles instead of making them."

Did Dada cough to hide his amusement while he put the turban in a box, which he then placed in a cupboard in an alcove to one side of the altar and closed the small door? "I think you should never miss a chance to serve The Supreme Lord. Everything we do should be for His satisfaction. You must appreciate how fortunate you are to have the opportunity to be His not your family's servant."

"Bapuji said Gopal and I are lucky because we are the first members of our family to have the chance to go to university."

"I was thinking of something less material."

"What?"

"Out of millions and millions of people, only one person has the chance to serve Sri Krishna, although, inspired by their spiritual leader, A. C. Bhaktisidanta Swami Prabhupada his disciples are spreading knowledge of the Supreme Lord all over the world."

"I'm sorry, I shouldn't have complained."

Her grandfather's smile expressed the unique sweetness of his character. "I'm glad you confided in me. If you're always honest, I can help you. If I found out you were dishonest, it would be as if I tried to help a ghost."

What was her grandfather's real meaning? She shivered and moistened her lips. sometimes his eyes seemed to look through her body at her inner being. What did he see at such times?

The front doorbell rang.

"Maybe Gopal's arrived," Dada said.

Indira noticed the gleam of pleasure in his eyes. "I'll find out."

He nodded.

She opened the front door and beamed at her brother. "Jai Shri Krishna. Are you okay?"

"Jai Shri Krishna, Indira. I'm so cold that I think we'll have a white Christmas."

At the mention of Christmas, she gazed into her brother's large, chestnut brown eyes fringed with lashes so long that she and Daisy envied them.

"What's the matter?" Gopal asked. "There are tears in your eyes."

"They still won't let me go to Daisy's for Christmas."

"I'm sorry, I know you'd really like to. But despite my attempt to persuade them, they refused."

"Thanks for trying."

Gopal shrugged. She took a parcel from him while he took off his coat. "Who is a spoiled boy?" Her warm tone expressing her love to amuse him instead of complaining because she couldn't accept the invitation.

"Little sister, I'm twenty-one, not a boy."

Why did he sound so annoyed? "Bapuji and Kaka are still at the warehouse, Dada's waiting for you to join him in the temple room, and Ba and Kaki are cooking."

He sniffed. "Whatever they are making smells good."

"Your favourite curries and sweet rice flavoured with cardamon."

"Your Siamese twin would enjoy the rice," he teased her, an affectionate twinkle in his eye.

"Who? Oh, you mean Daisy?"

His smile brightened his face. Happy, she studied him. Not only was he so handsome that girls turned to look at him in the street, but not one could ask for a better brother.

Ba came into the hall, embraced him, stood back, and scanned his face. "You have lost weight," she said anxiously.

"I hope so. No fried food, no curries cooked with ghee; no..."

"Gopal."

"I'm on a diet, Ba."

"A diet?"

"Yes, to keep my weight down."

"You're not fat."

"I will be, if I eat the too much food cooked with ghee."

Indira interrupted. "Don't be upset, Ba. He's teasing you."

"I'll pay my respects to Dada," Gopal said.

"Indira, make masala tea for your brother." Ba shook her head. "No, I'll make it. I know exactly how he likes it to be spiced."

The phone rang. Indira answered its summons.

"Who is it, Indira?" Ba asked.

"Daisy."

"Anyone would think that you and Daisy are joined at the hip," Gopal murmured.

Indira ignored his provocative comment and spoke to her mother. "Daisy's asking if I may go to the woods tomorrow afternoon with her to gather holly to decorate her house for Christmas."

Ba hesitated.

"Perhaps Dada would like some to decorate the altar," Indira suggested.

"I don't think so. It's prickly. Anyway, he prefers flowers," Ba said.

"Indira, If Ba agrees, would you like me to go with you and Daisy?" Gopal asked.

Happiness welled inside her. "I'd love you to come with us. We see so little of you these days."

"None of us do. He often comes home late or stays in London at night," Ba grumbled.

"I'll be at Daisy's house on Saturday. He could pick me up in the afternoon after we do our homework," Indira said before Ba could begin cross-questioning Gopal about why he often came home so late from London or stayed overnight with a friend.

"Very well." Ba gazed lovingly at Gopal. "He'll look after you and Daisy. The cold air will make you hungry. Invite her to have tea with us before she takes the holly home."

Indira arranged it with Daisy and put down the phone. "Daisy's mum will collect her after work today if that's okay with you, Ba."

"Before or after surgery to separate the two of you?" asked Gopal and smiled with laughter dancing in his eyes.

Indira pouted.

"Stop teasing her," Ba said half-heartedly.

Indira laughed and waved her forefinger at him. "If you don't obey, Ba might punish you."

* * *

Daisy narrowed her eyes as she plumped up a cushion in the lounge and wiped perspiration from her forehead with the back of her hand. "Um, we haven't got time to chat, I must sort the house for Mum before Gopal arrives."

"Why did you look at me like that?" Indira persisted.

"How did I look at you?" Daisy repeated.

"Funny peculiar, as your grandmother would have said."

Hugging the cushion, Daisy sank onto the sofa. "I had a nightmare about -. No, it was too terrifying for me to describe."

Indira sat next to her and put an arm around her shoulders. "It isn't. We always share everything."

"Though I was asleep I knew it was only a nightmare, but no matter how hard I struggled, it was almost impossible to wake up."

"What was it about?"

"You as...as a sati, screaming for help when the funeral pyre was lit," Daisy said in tears.

"Oh, Daisy. I know you're imaginative and squeamish. I'm sorry for telling you my great-great grandmother was a sati and described the...er...procedure. That's what triggered the bad dream. Forget about it. I'll help you finish the housework, then we'll finish our homework before Gopal arrives."

"I'm afraid I'll have the same nightmare again," Daisy whispered.

Indira squeezed her hand. "If you don't switch off the light and pray before you go to sleep, I don't think you will."

"Really?"

"Yes," Indira said firmly.

* * *

Daisy put the nightmare out of her head as she walked across The Green toward the wood with Indira, and Gopal, who pushed a wheelbarrow. Every moment the weather seemed to grow colder. She gazed up at the ominous grey sky and shivered in the chilly air, wound her wool scarf around her head and tucked the ends into her cosy coat. "I think it will snow."

"Probably," Indira shivered, "but I hope it won't before we go to my house."

"If it does, I shall make a snowman, with small stones for eyes, a carrot nose, and a strip of red apple skin for a mouth. And I'll wrap my old scarf around his neck. Gopal, tomorrow, would you help me make it in my garden?"

"I might, Daisy, if you were still a small child and asked me nicely," he teased her, and laughed. "Anyway, if I agreed wouldn't you find it too cold?" Gopal asked.

Daisy wriggled her fingers, glad of her warm gloves. "Not if I'm well wrapped up. Making a snowman is fun. Will you join in, Indira?"

Indira sniffed. "Fun? When it's freezing outdoors?"

Daisy linked arms with her. "Don't be a spoilsport."

"Very well," Indira said, grudgingly.

On the outskirts of the wood, Daisy wished, not for the first time, she was not an only child. "And we could have a snowball fight."

Indira and her brother shook their heads. "No," they said simultaneously.

Gopal jolted the wheelbarrow over uneven ground. "Why does it always seem colder in Cherminster than in London?" he muttered.

"I don't know, but I know Ba wonders why you come home late and often stay overnight in London. If she didn't know you would never get up to no good, she might be suspicious."

Gopal guided the wheelbarrow around the massive trunk of a fallen oak tree.

Daisy glanced at him. His cheeks looked rosy. Were they coloured by more than freezing air? "By the way, Indira, Mum wondered if you and Gopal would like to join us at the carol service in Cherminster Cathedral on Christmas Eve."

Indira exchanged a glance with Gopal, whose expression gave no clue to his answer.

"I'm sorry, we can't. You see, there will be a satsun at our house," Indira said.

"What is that?" Daisy asked.

"It's a prayer meeting where my family and guests sing songs of praise in the temple room," Indira explained.

Daisy stared hard at her friend. Of course, she remembered, satsuns were held in the afternoon. If they wanted to, Gopal and Indira would have time to come to the cathedral in the evening. She pressed her lips into a firm line. Although Indira had visited Cherminster Cathedral on a school excursion, did she feel uncomfortable in the massive, grey stone building? It was so majestic that she might have felt like an alien dwarfed by the tall pillars and lofty ceiling, and the solemnity in contrast to the lively temple in Letchmore Heath, where Indira's cousin married, and Daisy had visited twice.

Chapter Seven

"Daisy, do you know where the best holly bushes are?" Gopal asked.

"Yes, I'll lead the way to ones with loads of berries."

Their feet crunched on fallen autumn leaves as they walked in single file along a narrow path, edged with oak, sycamore, beech, hazel and rowan, their bare branches resembling black lace against the dull grey sky.

Gopal's forehead creased. "Daisy, I hope you don't walk here on your own. You might have an accident – fall over or something...er...nasty could happen to you. My parents would never allow Indira to come here on her own."

Or go anywhere else alone! "Our next-door neighbour, Mrs Bedmund, is too old to exercise her fierce Alsatian. Mum allows me to take him for walks in the Green and woods on most days because I'm safe with him. Don't worry, if I had an accident and couldn't get up, Mum would join a search party to find me."

Gopal's frown deepened. "Even if the dog attacked anyone who tried to harm you, I hope you don't come here after dark."

"No, of course I don't," she said appreciative of his concern. "Mum told me not to and I'm not stupid." The path widened. She pointed toward large holly bushes. "Bother! People have been here before us and cut the lower branches." She brandished her late grandmother's walking stick. "Gopal, if I hook the upper branches loaded with berries to pull them down, I think you're tall enough to cut some."

"I wondered why you brought the stick," he said.

She visualised her immaculate grandmother, holding it to steady herself. "And now you know," she replied pertly to hide her grief.

He bowed. "Your servant, ma'am."

Daisy giggled and curtsied. "Don't tease me, sir."

She took secateurs and a pair of tough gardening gloves out of a bag and handed them to him.

"I'm glad there are so many berries for the birds to eat." Daisy hooked a branch with the walking stick and pulled it down as she sang.

The holly and the ivy,
When they are both full
grown,
Of all trees that are in the
wood,

The holly bears the crown.

O, the rising of the sun,
And the running of the deer
The playing of the merry organ,
Sweet singing in the choir.

The holly bears a blossom,
As white as lily flow'r,
And Mary bore Sweet Jesus Christ
To be our dear Saviour.

O, the rising of the sun,
And the running of the deer
The playing of the merry organ,
Sweet singing in the choir.

"You have a beautiful voice." Gopal reached up and cut a branch loaded with jewel-bright red berries in contrast to prickly dark green leaves and handed it to Indira.

"Thank you for the compliment." If only she had a tall, handsome brother as nice as him.

"Daisy deserves it," Indira said to her brother. "She is in the school choir and was chosen to sing a solo in the Christmas concert."

"Congratulations." Gopal stood on tiptoe to reach more branches.

Daisy sang the next verse while she and Indira put them in the wheelbarrow.

The holly bears a prickle,
As sharp as any thorn,
And Mary bore sweet
Jesus Christ
On Christmas Day in the morn.

O, the rising of the sun,
And the running of the deer
The playing of the merry organ,
Sweet singing in the choir.

Tearful because it had been one of Grandmother's favourite carols, she wiped her closed eyes on the back of her glove. Startled by applause, she opened them and saw a well-dressed, middle-aged couple, with hats on their heads smiling at her.

"Bravo. Would you treat us to the next verse?" the gentleman asked.

Daisy noticed his white clerical band partly hidden by the scarf around his neck. She nodded. Maybe Grandmother could hear her from heaven and was proud of her, although pride was one of the deadly sins.

The holly bears bark,
As bitter as any gall,

*And Mary bore sweet
Jesus Christ
For to redeem us all.*

The strangers joined in the refrain, their voices mingling with hers soaring to the sullen sky in which grey clouds gathered.

*O, the rising of the sun,
The running of the deer,
The playing of the merry
organ
Sweet singing in the choir*

The clergyman scrutinized her. "Who would have thought I would find a star on a walk through the wood?" he murmured.

"What is your name?" his wife asked.

"Daisy Royston and these are my friends Indira and Gopal Nathwani."

The woman glanced at them. "How do you do?" She turned her attention to Daisy. "My dear, you sing like an angel. My husband, Reverend Paul, is the choirmaster at Cherminster Cathedral. Judging by his reaction to your voice, I presume he will invite you to sing sweetly in the choir."

"Yes, I shall." Reverend Paul pulled a notepad and pen out of his pocket, wrote something, tore out a piece of paper, and handed it to her. "A glorious, pitch-perfect soprano like yours is rare. Your voice is a heaven-sent gift. If you would like to join the choir, please ask your parents to contact me."

Overwhelmed by the opportunity to sing in one of England's famous cathedrals, Daisy gasped. Breathless, she stared at him. "Thank you, my father died," she explained regretfully," but I shall ask my mother for permission."

"I hope she will agree. God bless you, Miss Royston. May the light of His countenance shine upon you." Reverend Paul looked at his wife. "My dear, hold my arm. I don't want you to fall on the uneven path."

Miss Royston! No one else had ever addressed her as though she were an adult. Fizzing with excitement, she watched the couple saunter away. Was there any reason for Mum to refuse this excellent opportunity?

Enchanted by the image of herself in a choir stall dressed in a white surplice, Daisy smiled.

Indira hugged her. "Wow! An amazing opportunity for you."

"It is," Gopal agreed, "but I know little about choirs and think joining one would be a huge commitment."

Daisy came down to earth with a bump. Yes, it would, and after work, Mum would be too tired to drive her to and from the cathedral for rehearsals. Besides, Mum needed her help in the house, and homework took up a lot of time. Her initial enthusiasm waned. Did she really want to be part of the cathedral choir? Since her grandmother's death, she only went to church occasionally. Satisfied with her place in the school choir, she would refuse Reverend Paul's offer.

"Are you going to join?" Indira asked.

Certain the dedication required would be a burden, Daisy shook her head. "No, it would take up too much time,"

"Now that's settled, shall I cut more holly?" Gopal asked.

Daisy looked down at the pile of branches in the wheelbarrow. "There's enough unless you and Indira want to decorate your house."

"We don't follow that Christmas custom," Indira said. "I'm hungry. Let's have tea at our house."

Gopal took a step away from a tall holly bush. The jagged end of an old branch ripped the sleeve of his black, knee-length padded coat. He fingered it. "I should have worn an old coat instead of my new one." He grinned. "I can almost hear Ba scolding me for being careless."

Indira laughed before she spoke. "So, can I, but she loves you so much that she will forgive you anything."

He frowned. "I hope so," he said, very quietly as though he had something which worried him on his mind, but Indira didn't seem to notice he seemed abstracted.

"Anyway," she continued, "perhaps Ba can mend it. If she can't, you can buy another one." She patted her stomach. "Time to go. I'm hungry. I wonder what Ba and Kaki have made for tea."

Accompanied by birdsong and the sound of creatures rustling in the undergrowth, the freezing air stinging her nose and cheeks, Daisy led Indira and Gopal through the wood and across The Green to the Nathwani's house. "I'll put the holly in the boot of my car ready for me to take you home," Gopal said.

"We'll help you," Daisy said.

The holly crammed into the boot, the wheelbarrow parked in front of the back garden gate, they entered the large porch where they left their muddy boots before going indoors.

Grateful for the central heating, Daisy pulled off her gloves and shoved them into her coat pocket.

Mrs Nathwani bustled into the hall. "Tea will be ready as soon as I finish frying samosas filled with spiced peas and potatoes." She watched them take off their coats, looked closer, and frowned at Gopal. "Your coat's ruined." She admonished him with a wave of her hand. "You're not a child. You should be more careful. Besides, you should have worn your old one."

Indira exchanged an amused glance with Daisy that silently asked, 'What did Gopal say?'

"I know, Ba, and I'm sorry," Gopal replied as meekly as a penitent child. "I'll take it to my room."

"Wait, your Bapuji and Kaka want to speak to you. I'll clean your coat before I decide if it's worth mending."

"Don't fuss, Ba," Gopal chided her. "I'll take it to the dry cleaners and ask if it can be invisibly mended."

"There's no need." Mrs Nathwani laughed. "Invisible mending! I could never have guessed you know about that." She took the coat and handed it to Indira. "Go upstairs and put it into your brother's laundry basket, it must be washed before I decide what to do with it."

Daisy glanced at Indira's mother. Such a fuss about a torn coat!

Indira bundled the coat into her arms. "Come with me, Daisy to wash that dirty smudge off your face," Indira said.

Daisy peered into the large, gilt-framed mirror on the wall in the hall. "Oh no, I look a fright. My hair is a mess, and you're right, I must wash my cheek."

"Give me my coat," said Gopal, his voice brusque. "I'll take it upstairs,"

Indira smiled at him. "No, join Bapuji and Kaka."

* * *

In the bedroom, Indira checked Gopal's coat pockets. She took out a wallet, car keys, a small diary, a silver pen, and an envelope that had been opened. "I'll put these on his dressing table." On her way across the large room, she tripped over the edge of the oriental rug, and fell.

"Are you okay?" Before Daisy could help her, Indira scrambled up.

"I'm alright."

"Sit down to catch your breath." Daisy stooped to pick up photos which had spilled from the envelope onto the floor. She gazed at the first one, chuckled, and held it out toward Indira, who sat rubbing her knee. "Look at this photo of your brother and a beautiful girl. If your mother saw it, what would she say?"

Indira took it, evidently puzzled. Her eyes widened as she stared at it. "Ba would ask him who the white girl is. Even if Gopal said she is only a friend he met at college, Ba would cross-question him."

"I think she's Gopal's girlfriend." Daisy chuckled and handed more snapshots to her friend.

The first one depicted the girl holding hands with Gopal as they sat on the edge of a low wall around a pool with a fountain in its middle. In another one Gopal hugged her. In the third, his arm around her, the girl rested her head over his heart, her long, loose auburn hair spread from his chest to his waist.

Daisy gazed at another photo. "So romantic," she murmured.

Her breath catching in her throat, Indira ignored her best friend, who did not understand the trouble the photos would cause if the family saw them. She picked up the envelope and opened it with an unsteady hand.

"Are you alright?" Daisy repeated.

Indira shook her head. "How can I be after seeing these?"

"Why are you so upset?"

Indira's eyes blazed. "Gopal and I shouldn't keep secrets from our family. I've been warned many times not to talk to cheating boys, who would flirt, say they love me but not want to marry me. My brother is one. My family trust him and I can't imagine the consequences if they find out about -." The words choked in her throat as she brandished the photos.

Daisy sat down next to her on the floor and put her arm around her shoulders as she withdrew a letter.

"I don't think you should read your brother's letter," Daisy said.

"I must find out what's going on."

Her arm still around Indira, Daisy looked down and they read.

My darling Gopal, my only love for now and forever,

I'm already missing you and am counting the days until I see you and am telling myself that by then you will have told your family about us.
You can't imagine how much I miss you and look forward to spending more nights cuddling up in bed with you.
Without you I won't enjoy Christmas, but I must be cheerful, so I don't ruin the festive season for my parents.
I love you more than words can express and look forward to seeing you,

Your very own,
Scarlet.

"Our family would never agree to his marrying her and I'm sure Gopal wouldn't give us up for her." Silent tears ran down Indira's face. "I can hardly believe my brother is cheating the girl. If Ba and Bapuji find out Gopal shares a bed with that girl, they will be horrified. And, if they do, I dread hearing what Kaka and Kaki will say." She read the letter repeatedly. Her lips quivered. "And the shock might give Dada a heart attack. I can hardly believe Gopal is fooling Scarlet silly girl and us," Indira said with tears in her eyes.

"I don't understand?"

"If Gopal marries a white girl, I'm sure they will kick him out of the family."

"I can't believe you refer to her like that," Daisy shouted. "Mum and I judge people by their characters. not the colour of their skin. That makes you and your family racists."

Tears trickled down Indira's cheeks. "No, we're not. If we were, you wouldn't be welcome here," she said indignantly and brushed her tears away with the back of her hand.

"Don't cry." Again, Daisy put an arm around her.

"We're not racists! My family are proud of our traditions and culture. They want Gopal's wife to share them so she will fit in."

"Calm down. Surely when it comes to marriage, what your brother wants is most important."

"Yes, it is," Indira said. "I don't disapprove of a couple of men from or community and their English wives who made what are called mixed marriages. One of the wife's family disapproves as much as his. It must make their life difficult. As for the others, I think there's uneasy truce between the husband and the wife's families." She gulped. "Whatever my brother does in future, I'll always love him and hope he'll be happy."

Chapter Eight

On Christmas Eve, exhausted by ceaseless thoughts about Gopal's secret girlfriend, Indira swept and washed the marble floor in the temple room. When it dried, she made garlands with pink carnations imported from overseas for the deities to wear on Christmas Day. Kaki opened the door and rang the brass bell, to announce her arrival to the deities, Sri Krishna with a peacock feather tucked into his turban and Srimati Radharani with a wreath of flowers on her head.

Kaki gazed at the garlands spread out on the cloth. "They are beautiful. When I was a child, my mother taught me how to make them." She looked at her wristwatch. "Indira, it's time for you to help me and your mother."

In the kitchen, Indira put stainless steel bowls of seedless raisins, chopped dried figs, and small pieces of sugar candy on the breakfast bar and put some aside for Dada to offer to the deities for their lunch. She scowled, resentful because she rarely had any time to herself, and filled all the small bags, to be given to the guests when they left after gathering this afternoon for a satsun in the temple room.

About to leave the kitchen and decide whether to confront Gopal about Scarlet, her head drooped when Ba asked her to slice okra.

Ba scrutinised her. "You're very quiet. Has something upset you?"

Yes, I'm worried about Gopal, and agree with the daughter who helps her mother in the local corner shop who complained. 'Our families treat us Indian girls like slaves.'

"No, Ba, I'm okay," she fibbed.

"Good. Please prepare the okra and tomatoes for a curry."

Indira assembled the okra, a damp cloth, sharp knife, and a chopping board on the breakfast bar. If the vegetables were wet after being washed in a bowl of water it would spoil the curry, so she wiped each pod with the cloth then cut them into half inch rings. Okra curry was one of her favourites. Her mouth watered as she chopped the tomatoes.

"Are you looking forward to seeing your cousins this afternoon?" Kaki asked.

"Yes," she replied, but knew she sounded uncertain.

If only she had someone to confide in. Should she confront Gopal? She had replaced the photos and letter in the envelope and put it with the other items from his pocket on his dressing table. There was no reason for him to suspect she had discovered his secret. Should she tell her Dada or Bapuji about her brother and Scarlet? If she did, it would rock her family's foundation.

Indira prepared the dining room and helped to clean the kitchen. Head bent she loaded the dishwasher.

"Usually, you're talkative but you're very quiet today. Do you feel all right?" Kaki asked.

No, I don't. I want to talk things over with Daisy, but I won't see her for a few days, unless I get permission to visit her on Boxing Day. "I'm fine, thank you, Kaki."

"You haven't had much to say since you and Gopal gathered holly with Daisy," commented Ba, who noticed everything.

* * *

Indira distributed the little bags of sanctified dried fruit and candied sugar to ladies, their saris colourful as flowers in a summer garden. When the last guest went out into the cold, dark night, she put their empty glasses of juice into the dishwasher.

"Are you ill?" Ba asked anxiously. "You hardly said a word to anyone."

"Don't worry, I'm not sickening for anything."

"Ignore her. I think Indira's sulking because she can't spend Christmas with Daisy," Kaki said.

That rankled! Indira longed to be a little girl without any problems. She opened her mouth to retort and thought better of it.

Kaki poured the fragrant brew of spiced tea into cups and put them onto a tray. "Shall we relax at the breakfast bar before we cook?"

"Yes." Ba's back toward Kaki, she held up a hand and shook her head signaling to Indira not to speak.

She pretended not to have noticed the silent warning. "I'm not sulking, but so what if I want to spend Christmas at Daisy's house? I don't care what you say, Kaki. You're not a strict vegetarian and-"

Ba glanced at her sister-in-law. "Be quiet, Indira! That's a ridiculous accusation. Don't make trouble."

"I'm not the one making it, Ba. Why should I be quiet? She and Kaka are hypocrites. I'm not a child blinkered like a horse to keep me from seeing things. I know Kaki eats cakes with eggs in them which means she should not cook for the deities, and that Kaka drinks beer, spirits, and wine."

Ba sank onto a stool. "Is that true? How do you know?"

"I found the evidence when Bapuji gave me Kaka's car keys and asked me to fetch some files from the boot of his car."

"Hold your tongue," Kaki exploded.

Indira ignored her and Ba's shocked face. "As for Gopal-"

"Don't say a word against your brother," Ba interrupted.

"If you believe he's perfect, you're mistaken."

"Go to your bedroom and think about what you have said." Ba's eyes begged her not to say more that would shatter the household's peace.

In a tune familiar to Indira since she was a baby, Kaki's gold bracelets clinked together as she gesticulated, obviously outraged. "I won't tolerate this. I shall tell your Kaka what you accused us of," Kaki said her voice raised in anger.

Ba's chest heaved. "Indira never tells lies but maybe she has misunderstood something."

Kaki sniffed and hurried out of the kitchen rigid with anger.

"You shouldn't make trouble, there might be another explanation for what you discovered in your Kaka's car."

She shrugged. It's a good job Kaki interrupted me before I lost my temper and mentioned Gopal and Scarlet. I must speak to him about my discovery.

"It's not fair, Ba."

"What isn't?"

"You should trust me. If I spent Christmas at Daisy's, I wouldn't eat meat, fish, or eggs or drink alcohol."

Ba sighed, sat on a high stool at the breakfast bar and sipped her tea. Before she finished it Gopal entered the kitchen.

"Indira, Bapuji wants to speak to you in the sitting room." He coughed, then added. "Later, there's something I'd like to ask you about."

Her cheeks hot, she wondered if he guessed she saw the snapshots and read Scarlet's letter.

Ba looked at them. "What do you want to ask her?"

"Nothing important," Gopal said quickly. "I'll tell you later."

No, he won't if it's about Scarlet! Indira thought.

She entered the sitting room with Ba and Gopal where Bapuji, who sat there with Kaka and Dada, looked at her sternly. "Were you rude to your Kaki?"

Furious, she swallowed hard trying to hide her anger and didn't reply.

"If she'd gone to school in India as I recommended, the girl would know how to speak to us," Kaka said.

"Why should I respect you?" Her voice raised, she repeated what she knew about her aunt and uncle. "Kaka, you, and Kaki are such hypocrites that...that... I won't stay here. I'm going to Daisy and Mrs Royston to spend Christmas with them." Indira dashed out of the lounge and slammed the door. She snatched her padded coat from the stand. Without putting it on, she opened the front door and regardless of thick frost underfoot, she fled down the path at the back of the house toward the green.

* * *

Gopal looked at Dada whose lips were tinged with blue, not from the cold seeping into the warm hall.

"Did my granddaughter tell the truth? Pushpa, if it is true that you're not a vegetarian you know you should not cook food to be offered to the deities? Harish, do you drink beer and alcohol?" he wheezed. "Don't answer, your faces tell me it is. I've been blind. I must set a better example."

"But you have given us a perfect one," Bapuji said with tears in his eyes.

"If I did, your brother and his wife would not offend Sri Krishna by eating or drinking anything unacceptable to Him. They have cheated us, pretending to observe our principles, and cannot escape their karma for wrongdoing."

"I'm sorry," Kaka said. "From now on we will only eat and drink what is acceptable to Sri Krishna."

Dada pressed the palms of his trembling hands together. "We must not be angry with Indira. She's a good child. Find her, Gopal, and bring her safely home."

"Krishna, please protect my daughter." Tears trickling down her cheeks, Kumud handed Gopal his long, black, Kashmir coat. "Button it up. Don't catch cold, put on your hat and gloves, and wrap a scarf around your neck."

"Worry about my sister not me, Ba." Gopal looked at his grandfather. "Dada you've had a terrible shock. Please try to relax. I'll find Indira and bring her back."

* * *

Indira halted her frantic rush near the pond covered with ice that glittered in bright light from the full moon. From the corner of her eyes, she saw a group of lads either sitting or standing by the bench, drinking from bottles of beer, and talking about presents they wanted for Christmas.

She looked away from them, trying to catch her breath, before she headed toward Daisy's home.

Light from a window in a house on the fringe of the green almost blinded her.

A lad seated on the bench stood. "Gorgeous, have a drink with us."

Alarmed, she remembered Daisy telling her Mrs Royston warned her it would be dangerous to take the shortcut through the park when it was dark.

"Come 'ere." His hands stretched out to grab her, another lad approached her.

"Krishna!" she exclaimed. Frightened, she turned around to run away.

"Paki, where are yer going? Be friendly."

"I'm not a Paki." She hurried, slipped, and almost fell.

"Bloody foreigner! 'Aven't yer got any manners?" a third one shouted.

Like a machine wound up fast by a single key, the group ran toward her. Fear shuddered its way through her. "If yer not a Paki, what are yer?" one of them scoffed, his face ugly by moonlight.

They formed a circle around her. She tried to shove her way out of it. Rough hands pushed her backward and forward and hurt her. Terrified, she cried.

"Cry-baby wants her Mummy?"

"Paki, shall I kiss yer tears away?"

"What's yer hurry, gorgeous?"

"It's Christmas. Give me a kiss."

They jeered and egged each other on.

A lad held out a bottle. "'Ave a beer."

Clouds covered the moon. Indira couldn't see her tormentors' faces. She swallowed then forced herself to speak. "I never drink beer."

"Be friendly. Try one. If you do, we'll let you go." The lad held an open bottle out.

Indira took it but couldn't force herself to drink something unacceptable to Sri Krishna.

She tried to push her way to freedom between two boys, one of them grabbed the end of her plait and dragged her back into the middle of the circle.

"Please, let go of me." Tears rolled down her cheeks.

"Perhaps she isn't a Paki. Maybe she's a Red Indian. Hold on to her and I'll teach her a lesson, Jake," a short, fat lad yelled.

The others whooped. Tipsy, they danced clumsily.

"No, I'll teach her one. What should I do?" Jake asked and brandished the blade of his flick knife in front of her face.

A real-life nightmare! Why was it happening to her? "Krishna, save me," she screamed.

"Redskin squaw suffer if she no have drink and smoke peace pipe to prove she friend," Jake chanted.

His friends roared with laughter at his tomfoolery.

The silver blade flashed.

* * *

Gopal ignored the speed limit as he drove to the Royston's house.

Daisy opened the front door, a mince pie in one hand. "Hi, Gopal. What a welcome surprise, we didn't expect to see you this evening."

"Is Indira here?" he asked, too worried to waste a minute.

"Who's there?" Mrs Royston called.

"Gopal."

Daisy's mum came out of the kitchen. "Come in. Have a cup of tea and a homemade vegetarian mince pie. Do you think your family would enjoy them? Shall I give you some to take home?"

"No, no thank you. I'm sorry for disturbing you. I came to ask if Indira is here."

"No, she isn't."

"Has she been here this evening?"

"No." Mrs Royston's eyebrows twitched. "What's happened? Is something wrong?"

"We don't know where she is. I'm searching for her. Please phone my house if she turns up?"

"Yes, of course I will," Mrs. Royston said.

"Sorry for disturbing you. I must go," he said hastily.

Gopal returned to his car. Did Indira take the short cut through the green, then change her mind about coming here? Was she sitting on the bench by the pond deciding whether to come to the Royston's house or go home?

He drove fast, parked the car and as he walked across the slippery grass, heard someone scream Krishna. His sister's voice. She sounded terrified. "Sri Krishna protect her," he prayed as he ran, his heart pounding. Despite the intense cold, sweat formed on his forehead. Even when he suffered a verbal racial attack, he had never experienced such fear.

Voices whooped and chanted. "Red skin squaw drink, smoke peace pipe, be friendly."

Gopal ran as fast as he could the frigid air painfully assaulting his lungs. He reached a gang of raucous boys who danced clumsily in a circle and roared with laughter. He shouldered his way through them. One of them waved something long and black above his head.

Clouds sailed away from the moon, which illuminated his sister's horrified face. "Jake threatened to scalp me," she sobbed hysterically. "He's cut off one of my plaits."

Outraged, Gopal's fists bunched. His shoulders tightened. His beloved sister had been terrorised. A mindless bully had chopped off some of her beautiful thick, waist length hair. Outraged, he aimed a punch at Jake, who still waved his trophy above his head. Jake and two other louts grabbed at him. Without the satisfaction of punching Jake's face, he lost his footing.

"You bastard!" he roared as he fell on his back.

"Gopal," Indira screamed.

A disturbed bird squawked. Cherminster Cathedral bells pealed, calling Christians to a carol service before midnight mass to celebrate the birth of Lord Jesus, Christ the Prince of Peace.

Indira's severed plait fell to the ground and lay like a snake near Gopal's face.

Jake, pocketknife in hand, the blade pointing away from him lunged forward to seize Indira. She stepped backward. Gopal struggled to get up. Jake tripped over his foot and landed face down on top of him.

"Krishna," Gopal cried out.

Jake rolled off her brother. With a gloved hand he wrenched the bloody blade out of Gopal's chest. "Let's get away from here," he yelled. As though ghouls chased them, he and his mates fled to the wood.

Aghast, Indira knelt beside Gopal who no longer gazed at the moon. "I'm here. You'll be all right. Wake up. Talk to me," she babbled.

Impersonal moonlight revealed his handsome face. She had seen effigies in the cathedral. Gopal lay so still it seemed a master craftsman had carved him out of stone.

Surely her brother could not have left his body when he called out to Krishna. Her hand trembled as she held a finger beneath Gopal's nostrils. At first, she couldn't believe he wasn't breathing. "Stay here. Don't go away," she pleaded. "Open your eyes!" she begged, unable to accept his soul had left his body.

A dog barked and ran toward her.

"Come here, Rover," a man ordered.

Paws and feet crunched on the frost.

"What happened?" a woman asked.

Indira shuddered. "Jake murdered my brother." She sobbed.

"My God! You poor girl. Leave him be," the woman's said in a soft voice. "Let me help you to get up."

"No." Indira clutched Gopal's lifeless hand encased in a glove. Her tears flowed faster. She blamed herself for his death. If she had not rushed out of the house and ignored the warning not to take the short cut across the green in the dark, he would be alive.

"Wait with her, Denise, while I dial 999," the man said.

Two pairs of hands drew her to her feet. "Sit on the bench, while we wait for an ambulance and the police," Denise said.

Indira sat as though frozen in time until a siren shrilled. A police car stopped near her, and a policeman and woman hurried toward them.

Denise stood. "We heard the girl's screams and sent for you," Indira heard her say.

"What is your name?" the policewoman asked her.

"Indira Nathwani."

"What happened?"

"How old are you?"

"Fourteen."

The burly policeman looked down at them. "Miss Nathwani, who is the dead man?"

The question drove home the reality of Gopal's soul leaving his body. "M...my brother."

Sirens shattered the silence. Blue lights flashed. An ambulance and several police cars arrived.

Two men carried out a stretcher from the ambulance.

Police constables sealed the area with striped tape.

"Very young." The policewoman's words pierced her consciousness.

"Miss Nathwani is trembling from head to foot. Wrap her in a blanket." the policeman said to one of the stretcher bearers. "Miss Nathwani, we'll take you home."

The shock would give her grandfather a heart attack. She wept when she stood, a red blanket draped around her.

Chapter Nine

On her way home from the park, the hood of her coat over her head, Indira huddled in the back of the police car. Neither Constable Barclay, who drove it, nor Constable Ashley sitting beside him, the first police constables to arrive on the blood-curling scene of her brother's murder, spoke.

If only she had not run away, her brother would be alive. Memories crowded her mind. Four-years-old at a birthday party she told Gopal she wanted a balloon. 'Of course, you may have one,' he had said, looking up at a bunch suspended from the ceiling. He stood on a chair, reached up, and untied one for her. And he had always protected her. She remembered a cousin teasing her until she burst into tears. "Why are you crying?" Gopal asked her. After her brother had words with him, their cousin apologised and did not dare to plague her again. She had always adored her big brother. Now, the unthinkable had happened, and she was to blame for his murder.

The car stopped in the driveway at her house. The policeman and woman got out.

Constable Barclay opened the door for her. "Come with us, Miss Nathwani."

Reluctant to face her family she couldn't move.

"Miss Nathwani, you won't need to say a word," Constable Ashley said. "We will break the news about your brother's death to your parents."

And to Dada, Kaka, and Kaki. Krishna, please don't let Dada have a heart attack when they inform him.

"Please come with us," the policewoman continued. "Best get it over and done with."

Shocked to the core by her words, Indira stared at her. Gopal's sudden death would never be finished.

"Miss Nathwani, please get out of the car, now," Constable Barclay said.

Scared by the authoritative, tall, burly police officer's firm voice, she obeyed. Her legs shook as she walked along the garden path.

Barclay knocked loudly on the door.

Ba opened it. "Indira you're safe." Her face crumpled into deep lines. "Why are police officers with you."

"May we come inside?" Ashley asked as the others clustered in the hall.

"Yes, yes of course," Ba said hesitantly as she stepped aside.

Bapuji frowned. "Indira, you should not have run away. Gopal is looking for you. I'm glad you are safe but, Princess, why have police officers brought you home?" he asked, his tone sharp. "What have you done?"

Tears cascaded from her eyes. She bent her head unable to speak. What would her dear father say when a constable told him Gopal was killed?

Barclay cleared his throat. "May we come in, sir?"

"Yes, you may," Bapuji replied.

"I think everyone should sit down," Ashley said.

"This way." Dada pressed his hand over his heart when he led everyone into the sitting room. Except for Dada and the constables, they sat. Worried about Dada's health, Indira gazed at him.

Ba stood. "I expect fresh air has given Gopal an appetite. He'll be hungry when he comes home. Please excuse me, I must go to the kitchen to-."

A sob escaped Indira. Ba had already cooked Gopal's lunch, his last meal, earlier in the day.

Indira wiped her face with her hands. It would be better for her mother to hear the truth from her instead of a police constable. "Gopal will never come home again. He was-."

"Don't be ridiculous," Bapuji interrupted her. "Of course, your brother will give up his search for you and be back soon."

Too distraught to break the news, Indira lost her courage and could not speak.

Barclay cleared his throat. "There is no easy way for me to say this. I am sorry to tell you that your son is dead."

"I beg your pardon!" Kaka exclaimed. "Gopal dead? My nephew is...was...a healthy young man. What happened? A car accident? Was he driving too fast in a hurry to find his sister?"

"No, sir, there is no easy way to tell you the truth," Ashley said, her square face and blue eyes almost expressionless, she looked at Barclay.

"I am sorry to tell you Miss Nathwani witnessed her brother's murder," Barclay replied, his fists clenched and his face impassive.

Kaki took a box of paper handkerchiefs from the coffee table and handed it to her. "Indira, wipe your face. Stop crying. Tears won't help. Tell us what happened," she said, her voice choked.

A range of emotions on her loved ones' faces appeared as they waited for an explanation. Her throat closed. Still, she could not speak.

"My son murdered. Why?" Bapuji gasped. "There must be a mistake. Everyone liked him. Who would kill him?

"We don't know, Sir, but we will do our best to find out," Ashley said.

Tears oozed from Kaki's eyes. Dada sat silent his hand still pressed over his heart.

Kaka wiped his eyes with his handkerchief.

Ba sank from the chair onto the floor. She pulled the end of her sari over her head and rocked backward and forward. "My son murdered!" She glared at Kaka. "It's your fault. If Indira had not discovered the truth about you and your wife, she would not have confronted you and run away. And...and my son, my Gopal, my darling, would be alive."

Obviously puzzled, the police constables exchanged glances while Ba sobbed.

Indira dashed toward the door to go to her bedroom because she could neither bear her grief, nor witness her family's. Ashley blocked her way. "Please stay here, Miss Nathwani. We need you to make a brief statement."

"Why have you asked my granddaughter to remain here?" Dada asked, his face an inscrutable mask.

"Miss Nathwani witnessed the crime. We need her statement."

"My poor child!" Dada walked across the room and stood next to her.

Barclay took a biro and small notepad out of a pocket. "I shall record her statement, but I won't question her this evening. Tomorrow, she must come to the police station to have a formal interview. She is a minor so a responsible adult must accompany her."

Indira leant forward. The hood slipped off her head.

"I shall escort her." A head and a half taller than her, Dada looked down at her.

"Your hair!" he exclaimed. "What happened?"

"Jake threatened to scalp me. Instead, he cut off one of my plaits." A sob escaped her.

"Who is Jake?" Barclay asked.

For the first time Indira experienced hatred. "My brother's murderer. One of the boys in a circle around me who jeered and taunted."

Dada put his hand on her head. She choked back her rage and gazed up at him, grateful for the symbolic blessing, knowing whatever happened she would always have it.

"Tomorrow, I will bring my daughter to the police station," Bapuji said to Dada in an uneven tone.

Dada shook his head. "No, I have said I will take her. You don't need to undergo that ordeal."

When Bapuji bowed his head and put his hands over his face, Indira thought he would cry. She gazed up into Dada's golden-brown eyes. "What can we do?" she whispered.

"Nothing. But remember that according to our scripture, if Jake escapes justice in his present life, he will suffer the consequences in his next."

Barclay wrote something. "Who is what-is-his-name?"

"Krishna is God," Dada stated.

"Oh, um, I see. I assure you every attempt will be made to find the murderer and arrest him."

Indira visualised her beloved brother's lifeless body lying on the frost-covered grass with the blade in his chest while Jake and his friends ran away. Bile rose in her throat. She squared her shoulders. Fury consumed her. *I want to kill Jake.*

"There is another formality to be observed," Ashley began. "Miss Nathwani identified her brother at the scene of the crime, but because she is a minor, one of you must make a formal identification. After Miss Nathwani makes her brief statement, my colleague and we will leave."

Indira sat next to her mother, who wept without restraint. "Hush, listen to the constables." She dried Ba's face with paper tissues and smoothed her disheveled hair.

After Indira finished a brief description of what happened in the park, "Ladies and gentlemen," Barclay commenced. He cleared his throat. "You will be informed about the case as we investigate it and have an opportunity to discuss your concerns and expectations."

Indira clenched her fists so hard that her nails dug into her palms. *Case! To him, Gopal is no more than a case!*

"It is our custom for the deceased's body to be prepared immediately for cremation and for the funeral to take place on the next day," Dada explained. "When may we bring my grandson's body home?"

"I can't listen to this." Ba jerked free from Indira and stumbled out of the lounge before she could help her.

Barclay looked at the closed door. "I sympathise with you, sir. The pathologist made a preliminary examination at the scene of the crime. I presume he diagnosed the cause of death as a wound made by the blade of a flick knife still embedded in the victim's heart. The coroner will decide when the body may be released."

"In accordance with your family's beliefs and religious convictions he will do so as soon as possible," Ashley said.

Bapuji gulped. "The murderer must be caught. I offer a reward of five thousand for information leading to Jake's arrest."

* * *

Indira accompanied Dada to the front door where he said goodnight to the police constables. She returned to the sitting room with him and gazed at his face carved in deeper lines than before. He looked at each of them then spoke. "We love Gopal who has left an empty space in our lives that can never be filled, and we will miss him."

How can he speak so calmly?

Kaki opened her mouth to speak.

Dada silenced her with a gesture. He sighed. "It is natural to grieve, but don't forget we are Vaisnavas, who believe Sri Krishna is the supreme God, so we must adhere to His precepts. In the Bhagavadgita, spoken by Him, He promises that one who remembers Him at the moment of death will live with Him in his eternal abode, Goloka Vrndavan which is beyond all material universes." Dada's hands trembled a little, but he continued. "My dear grandson is blessed-"

"Blessed!" Indira exclaimed, the horror of Gopal's death still with her.

"Yes, Indira. The soul is immortal. With his last breath Gopal said Krishna so he is now living with Sri Krishna forever," he said, his voice hoarse.

Indira hurried to the kitchen, filled a glass with water, returned to Dada and gave it to him.

He smiled. "Thank you." He drank the water. "We must phone our relatives to tell them Gopal has left us. Tomorrow, the news will have spread throughout the community. Indira, you were a baby when our family and friends gathered here to mourn your grandmother for thirteen days, but I know you will be brave and helpful while we receive those who come for the same period. Now, I must attend to our deities."

From then on anger sustained her while her mother retreated into impenetrable grief during which she only ate or drank a little when Indira begged her to. Every day, Indira sat next to her in the temple room while

Dada read from the Bhagavadgita to those who gathered to respect her brother. Outside their house, newspaper reporters gathered like a coven of avaricious crows. In town people gathered outside the police station to demand the murderer's arrest. On the third day after Gopal left his body – a term she preferred to death because the soul never died – Bapuji announced during a television broadcast that he offered a reward of five thousand pounds for information leading to the apprehension of the youth who killed her brother.

"Vulture!" Indira slammed down the phone in response to yet another reporter who offered a large fee in exchange for an exclusive interview. Dry-eyed from the time she woke in the morning until she went to bed in the evening, she concealed her anguish until the eighth day after the tragedy when the coroner released Gopal's body, and Bapuji paid an extortionate sum for it to be cremated on the next day.

While Kaki and other ladies prepared her brother's body for cremation, Indira's tears flowed again while she strung a garland of fragrant jasmine Bapuji had ordered from India. When she finished it, Kaki arranged it on Gopal's corpse in the coffin placed on a trestle table in the lounge. There, his family and those who came to mourn him would walk around it to make their last farewell before the lid was nailed down and it was taken to the crematorium.

Indira stood in the hall next to Bapuji, his face drawn into deep lines, near the front door to admit those who came to offer their condolences. He greeted them, Kaka took their coats, and escorted them to the temple room where Dada read the Bhagavad Gita aloud, then returned as Mrs Royston and Daisy stepped into the hall.

"Please accept my condolences," Daisy's Mum said. "We sent a card to express them but decided we should offer them in person."

"Indira! I can't believe it," Daisy exclaimed. "Nine days ago, we gathered holly with Gopal and now-" her lips quivered. Tears flooded her eye. She sobbed.

"Daisy, you promised to be brave," her mum said gently.

Daisy's arms around her, the dam that controlled Indira's devastation and fury burst again as they wept, their faces against each other's shoulders.

Someone knocked on the door.

"Girls, I sympathise with you but please stop crying and let go of each other," Mrs Royston said. "Mr Nathwani, should I take them to the lounge while you see who has come?"

"Not the lounge, the coffin is there," Bapuji and Kaka said simultaneously. "The dining room."

"Let go of each other," Mrs Royston said. "Come along."

Sniffing and crying, Indira entered the room and sank down onto a chair.

Mrs Royston took a small packet of paper tissues out of her handbag. She handed one to her and another to Daisy. "Blow your noses and dry your eyes. All the tears in the world won't bring Gopal back."

Indira's shoulders heaved but she stopped crying and wiped her face.

"Where is your mother, Indira?" Mrs Royston asked. "I must commiserate with her."

"She can't face anyone, so she is in her bedroom waiting to take leave of my brother before his funeral," Indira replied, almost choking on her distress.

Mrs Royston seemed taken aback. "How will she do that?"

Indira gulped. "It is the custom to walk around Gopal's coffin to pay respects and make silent, private farewells." Her voice betrayed that she dreaded seeing Gopal's lifeless face. "If you and Daisy want to, you may follow our tradition and, afterward listen to my grandfather lead everyone in prayer and read the Bhagavadgita in the temple room."

"We will, and we shall attend his funeral," Mrs Royston said. "When will it be held?"

"Tomorrow, but you can't attend it. In the past women never attended cremations. Dada decided we must observe the custom," she babbled.

Mrs Royston dabbed her eyes with a tissue. "Sweetie, the ordeal will soon be over, and, in time, you can put the tragedy behind you."

Indira straightened her back. "Never! I was there when my brother, who I will always remember, was murdered."

Bapuji entered the dining room. "Indira your mother is ready. Come to the lounge."

She trembled when she walked around the coffin, her head covered with the end of her sari, her hands pressed together. The last people to follow in everyone's footsteps were Mrs Royston, and Daisy, who, at the sight of Gopal's face, exploded into loud sobs and clung to her mum. Indira and Dada followed Mrs Royston as she guided Daisy into the dining room.

"Daisy, look at me and listen. Gopal's immortal soul lives on," Dada said. "At Christian funerals, the words dust to dust and ashes to ashes are spoken. Gopal's body will be cremated. His ashes will be sprinkled on our sacred river, the Ganges."

"I am sorry. I didn't mean to...to. But-." Daisy let go of her mum.

"You are shocked," Dada said quietly.

Mrs Royston looked at Dada. "I am surprised by your mention of Christian funeral services."

"I went to a Church of England school."

"Ah, that explains it." Mrs Royston put her arm around Daisy's shoulders. "I apologise for my daughter losing control. Before we leave, I repeat my sincere condolences to you and your family and-"

she broke off startled by a loud rat-a-tat-tat on the door.

Indira opened it and beckoned to Ashley and Barclay.

"Miss Nathwani, sir, good evening," Barclay said. "There are so many cars parked on your drive and outside your house on the road that I assume you have many guests. I apologise for my intrusion." He looked at Daisy and Mrs Royston. "I have good news for you and your family. Would you prefer to speak to us in private?"

"No, thank you, the lady is a close family friend, and the young lady is her daughter, Daisy," Dada's calm voice did not betray the impatience revealed in his eyes.

"Very well, sir. One of the youths present at your grandson's murder claimed the reward your son offered. The gang of underaged teenagers have been interviewed. Jake Symonds has been arrested."

"May he rot in hell!" Daisy exclaimed.

"Shush, Daisy." Mrs Royston looked at Ashley "I hope he will receive a life sentence for his senseless crime." She wiped tears from her eyes. "Everyone who met Gopal liked him."

Indira remembered the circle of beer-fueled thugs in a circle around her, their rough hands which pushed her back when she tried to escape, her severed plait waved in the air and witnessing Gopal's murder. Engulfed by grief, her knees buckled. Mrs

Royston grabbed hold of her to prevent her falling onto the parquet floor.

"I don't want to add to Miss Nathwani's -er -distress. I shall return tomorrow to-" Barclay said.

"Not tomorrow. That is when the cremation will take place. On the following day," Dada said.

Part Two

Chapter Ten
June 1974

Indira followed Mrs Lester, the school secretary, to the headmistress' large office, with its oak panelled walls and oak parquet floor.

"Miss Davidson, Indira Nathwani is here to see you." Mrs Lester announced.

Why have I been summoned? Indira thought when the secretary closed the door behind her.

Miss Davidson scrutinised her. Apprehensive, Indira gazed out of the large sash window at the playing field.

"Indira, please be seated."

She perched on the edge of a chair opposite the large, tidy desk, with in and out trays, her hands clasped tight on the lap of her summer uniform, a spring green and white checked dress.

Miss Davidson finished reading what looked like a letter, then put it down on the desk next to her silver fountain pen.

Indira moistened her lips with her tongue and fidgeted. What would her principal say?

Her short sandy-coloured hair in perfect order, the jacket of her grey suit immaculate, Miss Davidson, a small but commanding figure gazed at her. "Indira, your marks have dropped this year."

Not sure if she should say something, Indira nodded.

"If I didn't know you've been through a terrible ordeal, I'd be disappointed because you were one of my most promising pupils."

So, what if I was a promising pupil? No one can understand what I've been through.

"Indira, I sympathise with you and have your best interests at heart. Now the trial is over, and it is nearly the end of the summer term, I think you should repeat this year."

At home, life without Gopal blighted the atmosphere. Giving testimony in court had forced her to relive the horror of those young louts' abuse, and the trauma of her brother's murder. She remembered her furious indignation when Jake Symonds had only been convicted of manslaughter because he had not intended to kill her brother. Frustrated by the injustice, she wanted to cry.

Miss Davidson's voice intruded on her misery. "I haven't spoken to your father for some time."

Before Gopal left his body, Bapuji embarrassed her because she was certain he was the only father who phoned her principal every week to ask about his daughter's progress.

"He's very busy," she mumbled.

"I'm sure he could find time to discuss your education," Miss Davidson said in an even tone.

Indira couldn't think of anything to say before the principal continued. "If you don't repeat the year, you might not catch up sufficiently to go to university after you sit your O and A levels."

She caught her lower lip between her teeth so hard that she winced. Since her brother left his body prematurely, she doubted Bapuji cared about either her results or future.

Her small, square hands with short nails together on the tidy desk, Miss Davison scrutinised her. "Don't worry, your father told me he wants you to continue your education after you leave school."

After Gopal left his body or before?

"Don't be disheartened. Tell your parents I and your teachers understand the last six months must have been... um... difficult. Before I speak to your father, please tell me what you think of my suggestion."

Indira shrugged. What could she say? How could she explain the void in her daily life since Gopal died? As for her poor marks – she should have concentrated and worked harder.

"Very well, Indira, even if you've nothing to say, please remember I'm always here to encourage my pupils. In future, if you want to speak to me about anything, anything at all, ask my secretary to make an appointment for you to see me."

"Thank you."

"You may go," Miss Davidson said.

In the outer office Indira ignored Mrs Lester's smile and returned to the corridor where Daisy waited for her during break.

"What did she want?"

"For me to repeat a year."

Daisy linked arms with Indira. "Come on, we've missed our bus. If we hurry, we won't miss the next one."

Indira blinked. Previously I would not have been allowed to catch the bus home. My life has changed for the worse in every way.

They marched past the changing room with its long rows of grey metal lockers and scurried down a short flight of steps made hollow in the centers by several generations of footsteps. Outside, sunshine bathed them.

What would I do without Daisy's friendship, sympathy, and support? We sit next to each other in class, share our notes, and packed lunches. Sometimes she even makes me laugh and, for a moment, forget how unhappy I am.

"Daisy, I won't!"

"What, Indira?"

"I won't repeat the year. I'll have tuition during the holidays." She ran back into the school.

"Wait for me," Daisy called, and followed her friend to the secretary's office.

Indira rapped on their headmistress' door. Instead of waiting for permission to enter, she opened it. "Miss Davidson, I don't want to repeat the year! I'll have tuition and work hard to catch up."

"Very well, Indira. If you work hard, I think you can catch up."

"Thank you, thank you very much, Miss Davidson, I want to go to university."

"Good, I am sure you will be a credit to the school."

* * *

Indira let herself into the house with her own key given to her when Bapuji told her to come home on the bus unless Mrs Royston brought her home. She dumped her schoolbag near the door as Dada came into the hall.

"You're late, I was anxious."

She never wanted to worry him. "I'm very sorry, Dada."

"Where were you?"

Thank goodness! Someone still cared about her in this gloomy house.

"The headmistress sent for me."

"Why?"

"Because I'm not doing well."

"Never mind. I know you can do better."

"I'll try to." She smiled at him, grateful for his encouragement.

Upstairs, she changed into a pale blue tunic, and dark blue trousers. When she came downstairs, she went to the kitchen where Dada sat at the breakfast bar.

"Shall I make you some fresh orange juice?"

"No, thank you, Indira. Have your tea."

In companiable silence he waited for her to prepare spiced tea boiled with milk. When it was ready, she removed the tight-fitting lid from a tall, round, steel container from a cupboard and took out some readymade, vegetarian biscuits.

She sat opposite him. "Is Ba still resting?" she asked, aware of the forlorn note in her voice.,

"Yes."

"Would you like a cup of tea and something to eat?"

"No, no thank you, Indira."

"Do you think Ba has a headache?"

"Maybe."

She heaved a sigh. Since Gopal left his mortal body, Ba spent most of her time in bed. "After my tea I'll make supper."

"Shall I help you?"

Indira smiled at Dada again. What would she do without him, the only member of the family who never said a harsh word to her since she ran into the park on that dreadful evening.

"What are you going to make?" Dada asked.

"Dahl, aubergines stuffed with spices, chapatis and rice."

"I expect your kaki will be home in time to help you make chapatis."

"Yes, I expect she will."

Indira moistened her lips with her tongue. She and Kaki only spoke to each other when necessary, and Kaki frequently went out and left many tasks to her,

"I'll fetch our deities' plates for you to put portions of the meal on for me to offer it to them." Dada's walking stick tapped on the tiled floor as he walked slowly to the door. Her eyes damp, she watched him. Before the tragedy, he walked straight-backed without a prop to steady him.

Indira finished her tea and cleared the breakfast bar. She put dull yellow split lentils into a bowl of warm water. Indira rubbed them with hare hands, changed the water and repeated the process until the water remained clear. Indira put them in the pressure cooker and added water to cook them until they were a pulp.

She diced the halved aubergines without cutting through them and mixed the spices for the stuffing. Next, she chopped tomatoes and chilies separately, grated ginger, shredded fresh coriander leaves and assembled spices for the dahl. Light brown, fragrant powdered coriander and cumin, bright yellow turmeric, chili powder the colour of terracotta, salt, and sugar.

"You haven't done much," Kaki grumbled as she entered the kitchen and looked around.

"I came home later than usual."

"I suppose you were with Daisy. I wish you had never met her. If only her mother hadn't invited you to spend Christmas with them Gopal would be alive," Kaki said her face and voice sour as lemons.

Indira pressed her lips together. She wanted to finish cooking, eat her meal, and ask her father to arrange tuition.

Kaki slammed two large tins of mango pulp onto the table. "Your mother's useless. We must eat some readymade food until it's legal for you leave school and take over all her duties."

That decision is for Bapuji not you to make. She refused to reveal how much her aunt annoyed her, but she wouldn't allow the woman to criticise her mother. "Kaki, I always thought Ba did too much for us. She's earned a rest."

"Don't answer back, Indira. You've already caused enough damage to this family."

Indira added mustard seeds to melted ghee. When they crackled, she concentrated on adding the spices. She tipped in the dahl and stirred it vigorously as though she was trying to banish misery from the house.

How much more of Kaki's hostility could she put up with? Did her aunt think she hadn't loved Gopal as much as she did? Didn't she and the rest of her family know he was always in her thoughts? Didn't her parents love her anymore? Didn't her aunt and uncle love her? Kaki criticised her, and instead of pampering her as he did in the past, Kaka ignored her. These days he never gave her extra pocket money or asked her how she was getting on at school. Well, that might be her fault. She should not have mentioned he and Kaki were not strict vegetarians before she fled, and Gopal searched for her. No! She would not blame herself for her brother's death. Jake Symonds was to blame. Her legs trembled. She wanted to escape from Kaki, who irritated her like a gnat.

"Kaki, the curry is ready. Please add coriander to the dahl when it is almost ready and make the rice and chapatis while I look after Ba."

Indira went upstairs to the darkened room where her mother lay with a damp cloth on her forehead.

"How are you, Ba."
"What do you want?"
"Would you like some tea?"
"No."
"Some juice?"

"No. Only water."

She wished the doctor could help her mother. Bapuji said he might take Ba to India because a visit to a place of pilgrimage might help her. Perhaps it would. Maybe bathing in the sacred River Ganges would wash away some of her mother's sorrow. Would she feel better far from this house crowded with memories of Gopal?

Indira picked up the carafe from the bedside table, filled a glass with water and put it in her mother's hand. Its thin, claw-like appearance with prominent veins shocked her. Ba's plump, smooth hands used to be constantly busy. Now, her gold rings were loose.

"Fetch the paracetamol."

"No, Ba. I'm sure you take more than the maximum dose."

"What does it matter? What does anything matter now my Gopal is dead?"

"It matters to me. Please get up and teach me how to make samosas? Neither mine nor Kaki's taste as good as yours."

Ba looked away from her. "How can you be so cruel? Samosas were one of Gopal's favourites."

"I like them and want you to make some for me." Indira also wanted to say, I need you to collect Daisy and me from school when Mrs Royston can't. Please come back to us. Don't you love me enough to try? "I'll bring a tray up for you when dinner's ready," she muttered.

Ba fumbled under her pillow.

"Are you trying to find your tissues?"

"Yes."

Indira pulled the packet out and handed one to Ba, who wiped her eyes and blew her nose. Indira took the tissue between her thumb and middle finger and put it in the bin in the ensuite bathroom.

She removed the packets of paracetamol for fear her mother would swallow an overdose by mistake or-? She shuddered, unable to complete the thought.

* * *

Indira served the meal, ate with the family, then cleared up, her depression increasing until she had to force herself to speak to her father in Dada and Kaka's presence in the lounge.

Bapuji glared at her. Indira caught her lower lip with her teeth on the sore spot from when she caught it earlier in Ba's room. She wished her father's large, dark brown eyes would light up whenever he saw her as they did in the past, and she longed for him to call Princess.

"What do you want?" he asked.

She held out the packets of paracetamol. "Bapuji, I took these from your bathroom because Ba takes too many. I'm frightened she'll take an overdose."

He picked up his newspaper. "Put them on the coffee table, then leave."

Indira hesitated.

Her father cracked his knuckles, a familiar sign of displeasure. "Have you something else to say?"

"Yes, Miss Davidson sent for me."

"Why?"

She stared at the intricate pattern on the antique rug in front of the fireplace. To be calm, she tried to count the number of blood-red squares on its outer border.

"Well, what have you to say, Indira?"

How would he react? She must not be intimidated by his indifference. "I can't concentrate since...you know. My marks are poor. Miss Davidson wants me to repeat a year. I said I can catch up if I have a tutor in the summer holidays."

Her father stroked his upper lip with the forefinger of his right hand.

"Please may I have one, Bapuji."

"No, during the holidays, you'll be needed at home to look after your mother."

"Govinda," Dada reproached him.

Bapuji cracked his knuckles again. "Yes?"

"I suggest you accept the offer from Kumud's widowed sister to look after your wife, help to cook and manage the house."

"Very well, if you think it's for the best."

Indira sagged with relief. Her maternal aunt always treated her kindly.

"Indira, you may have tuition, but it's unimportant whether or not you do well at school," Bapuji said.

Why? Previously he'd always encouraged her to do her best and expected her to achieve the highest marks in class for every subject.

"Your father and I have discussed your future," Kaka said. "At sixteen you'll leave school and at eighteen marry a man we can train to take over the business when we retire."

"But...but I want to go to college or university."

"What you want isn't important now that Gopal has left his body," Kaka declared.

She glanced at Dada hoping he would intervene. "I could manage the business, Kaka."

"No, we want you to marry and, we hope, have sons."

"No one can force me to marry."

"Don't be dramatic, Indira," Bapuji scolded. "We'll arrange for you to meet suitable young men. You may choose the one you like best."

Put like that, it sounded reasonable, but it was not. She didn't want to marry when she was eighteen.

"Don't look so worried, child," Dada intervened and looked sternly at Bapuji and Kaka. "Pray to Lord Krishna. He always protects His devotees."

"If that is true, why did He allow Gopal to be murdered?" she said, voicing the question in her mind for a long time.

Her father's breath hissed like a snake's. His fists bunched. For a moment, she thought he might uncoil himself from his chair and strike her for the first time in her life.

Oh no. Kaki had entered the room in time to hear her question. "How could you ask that?" she shouted.

Dada stood. "Only Sri Krishna knows who His devotees are." He pressed the palms of his hands together, raised them to the level of his chest and faced them. "Indira always asks intelligent questions. The answer is that karma is complicated. We know that for every action, good or bad, there is a reaction. Only Sri Krishna knows why Gopal left his body, but I know those boys who tormented Indira, and the one who cut off her plait and was responsible for my dear grandson's death will reap as they sowed in this life or a future one." He smiled. "Indira, you're tired. Please go to bed and dream about Sri Krishna."

"I wish I could dream about Him," Indira whispered.

Dreams of Gopal woke her several times during the night. Her brother joked with her, took her out, bought her sweets or helped her with her homework. At the end of each dream she woke, turned over and tried to sleep again. Toward dawn she dreamt about his murder. Awake, her pajamas soaked with perspiration, her eyes gritty, she grimaced. "I can't stand it here. I really can't stand it!"

she exclaimed as she got up, showered, and dressed.

She went downstairs to the temple room where Dada had already woken the deities, served their morning sweetmeats, dressed them in sumptuous purple and gold silk, and adorned them with jewelry and flower garlands. Indira rang the temple bell. She folded the palms of her hands together and approached the altar, her mind uncontrollable as the wind.

After four or five minutes, she stood in front of Dada careful not to stand with her back to Sri Krishna and Srimati Radha Rani. He stopped reading The Bhagavadgita and gazed at her. "Jai Sri Krishna," he greeted her and smiled.

"Jai Sri Krishna, Dada."

Indira bit her lip and looked at the peach veins on the cool marble floor while he waited patiently for her to speak.

"Yesterday, you spoke so calmly about Gopal and karma. Don't you grieve for him?"

"I do, but I try to practice my faith. We must leave this material world, so I strive to be a wise man and accept happiness and distress equally."

"I wish I could be like you. You're so strong in your belief, so peaceful and kind."

"Thank you for your praise. If you strengthen your faith in Sri Krishna and always remember Him, you can be tranquil no matter what happens." Dada glanced at his gold Swiss watch.

Indira stooped to touch Dada's feet. "Please give me your blessings, regardless of whatever I decide to do in future," she requested, and wondered if she would be brave enough to carry out her plan tonight.

Chapter Eleven

The doorbell shrilled through the quiet house. Startled, Daisy put her mug of hot cocoa on the coffee table.

"It's after ten, who has come at this time of night?" Mum asked.

Daisy put her mug on a coaster on the coffee table. "I'll find out."

"No, I'll see who has come." Mum put her mug down, stood and tightened the belt of her warm dressing gown.

Daisy followed her into the hall.

The safety chain in place, Mum opened the door and peered out. "Who is there?" she asked, looking outside through the narrow space.

"It's me," a choked voice replied.

"Who?" Mum asked.

"Indira."

Mum removed the chain and pulled the door wide open. "Good gracious, Sweetie, what brings you here in the dark when rain is bucketing down. You're soaked." She stepped back.

Daisy turned on the hall light. Shocked, she and her mother stared at Indira's sodden, padded jacket and untidy short hair from which rainwater dripped down her face.

"Come in before you drown." Mum looked at the doorstep. "Daisy, bring Indira's suitcase and schoolbag indoors."

"I'm sorry, Mrs Royston, I know I shouldn't have come here, but I couldn't think of anywhere else to go."

"I'm glad you reached here safe and sound." Mum gripped Indira's hand and drew her into the hall. "Take off your jacket. Come into the kitchen, I'll make a hot drink for you."

Daisy dumped the wet suitcase and schoolbag on the floor.

Indira sank onto the bottom step of the stairs, buried her face in her trembling hands and wept.

"Hush, Sweetie. Get up, take off your jacket and come into the kitchen. You'll feel better when you're warm and dry with a hot drink inside you," Mum said.

Daisy couldn't think of anything to say or do to help her best friend.

Elbows on her knees, her hands on her cheeks, Indira wept.

Mum removed Indira's hands from her face. "Daisy, the poor girl's ice cold. I'll take her upstairs to your bedroom where she may dry herself and change her clothes. Tonight, she is welcome to sleep on the sofa bed." She tutted. "Get up, Indira. When you're comfortable, please tell me why you came here."

Indira ignored Mum, so they heaved her to her feet and Mum put an arm round Indira's waist to steady her.

"Daisy, fill two hot water bottles and make a piping hot, sweet drink for your friend and bring them upstairs."

Daisy hurried to the kitchen, filled the electric kettle, switched it on, and put some cold water into two hot water bottles. so, they wouldn't burst when she poured boiling water into them. She remembered Indira's mother and aunt believed spiced tea had restorative properties, so she made some, and added extra sugar. Careful not to spill any tea, she took the full mug of the piping hot brew and the hot water bottles, encased in fleece covers, upstairs. In her bedroom, she put them on the dressing table.

"I lit the gas fire because Indira's very cold," Mum said.

Daisy gazed at Indira, who sat on a yellow chintz cushion on the white wicker bedroom chair, her face covered by her hands as she sobbed.

Mum held out the mug of tea. "Drink this while it's hot to warm the cockles of your heart." She offered Indira two tablets. "Wash these down your throat with tea."

Indira removed hands from her face and stopped crying. She took the mug but didn't drink as she gazed at the small, white tablets. "What are they?" she whispered.

"Paracetamol."

"I don't want them. Ba takes too many."

"Don't worry about that. Only two will settle you, but they won't harm you. Please, pop them into your mouth and swallow them with your tea," Mum said in a gentle but firm voice.

As though she were a small, obedient child, Indira put them in her mouth. She gripped the mug with both hands. They trembled so much that tea slopped down her.

"I'm sorry, I'm sorry, I shouldn't have come here, I'm nothing but a nuisance to everyone," Indira quavered.

"Don't cry, Sweetie, spilt tea doesn't matter. Drink the rest while it's hot. Daisy, please fetch Indira's suitcase and schoolbag and I'll make up the sofa bed."

Daisy fetched them and helped her mother to prepare the bed. Mum tucked the hot water bottles under the top sheet, blankets, and cream candlewick bedspread. Then she helped Indira undress and wear the white silk nightdress Daisy found in the suitcase.

"Time to get into bed, Sweetie," Mum said. "Daisy, change into your pajamas, it's a school day tomorrow."

Snug in bed, shocked by Indira's misery, Daisy tried to think of something comforting to say. She watched Indira's tear-stained face, which looked sallow in the soft light cast by the bedside lamp. Mum had left it on in case Indira woke up frightened at night.

Nothing's been the same since Gopal died, but how could it be? Her eyes damp, Daisy slept.

* * *

What's that noise? Half awake, Daisy yawned and squinted at Indira, who stood by the door, her suitcase beside her on the floor. Daisy rubbed her gritty eyes, sat, and pulled down her rumpled pajama top.

"Sorry for waking you. I tried to be quiet," Indira mumbled.

"That's okay," Daisy said, relieved because her friend had a grip on herself.

"I shouldn't have come here last night." Indira grasped the small handle of her suitcase. "I must go. Please thank your mum for putting me up for the night."

"Where are you going?"

"Back to my house."

Before Indira went home, she should speak to Mum. "First have breakfast."

"I'm not hungry," Indira said, but put down the suitcase.

"Sit down." Daisy patted the edge of her bed. "What's wrong? Why did you come here?"

"I couldn't think of anywhere else to go."

"Oh dear," Daisy murmured, seeing tears flood Indira's eyes The mattress dipped as her friend sank down onto it. Bent over, Indira put her arms around her knees and pressed her head on them.

Daisy patted her back. "Please tell me what has upset you so much that you left home."

Indira's nose dripped. She wiped it on a tissue.

"We've always told each other everything. Tell me what's happened, Indira. I won't repeat it," Daisy promised, and gazed at her mother who had entered the bedroom without a sound.

"Only m...my gr...grandfather is k... kind to me and... and now they w...want me to marry when I'm eighteen. They plan to tr...train my husband to manage the business while I stay at home and have a son. And although I worked hard with a tutor during the summer holiday and don't need to repeat a year, they don't think my education is important."

"That's dreadful, no wonder you ran away." Since Gopal's death Daisy realised that Indira's family, which she once admired, was never all it seemed to be. She gazed at her mother hoping she would say something that would help Indira.

"Sweetie," Mum began, "after you went to sleep, I phoned your father to tell him you are safe. He thanked me and agreed you may stay here for as long as you want to."

Indira's lips quivered. "Thank you, Mrs Royston, I would like to stay here."

"That's settled, but remember whenever you are ready, I shall take you home. And Daisy."

"Yes, Mum?"

"Time to get ready to go to school. Hurry up, darling, I don't want you to be late on the first day of term. I'll write a note to explain Indira is staying at our house and will be absent today."

* * *

Almost ready to go to school Daisy brushed the tangles out of her curly blonde hair and watched her friend who lay in bed. "Indira, put on your dressing gown and come downstairs to have breakfast."

"I'm not hungry."

Her back toward her, Indira stood gazing out of the window and neither heard nor saw Mum quietly enter the bedroom. She put a finger against her lips and gestured to Daisy to follow her.

"Indira will eat when she wants to," Mum said in the kitchen. "Is everything you need in your school bag?"

"Yes, I packed it yesterday, but I won't know exactly what I need to take every day until I'm given this term's timetable."

"Good, sit down and eat your breakfast."

"I only want a drink."

"Don't go to school with an empty stomach."

Mum believed everyone should start the day off with something substantial to eat. She poured a glass of orange juice, put muesli in a white bowl ringed with blue, and added a dessert spoon of local honey to it. From a jug that matched the bowl she poured milk onto the cereal. "To please me, finish this."

Upset by Indira's misery Daisy had lost her appetite, but managed to sip half the juice and eat some muesli before she pushed the glass and bowl aside. Except for Indira's grandfather, Indira's family blamed her for Gopal's death. They needed help to come to terms with it. I don't because Mum helped me to accept that bad things happen to good people.

Daisy remembered those dreadful days before the boys were arrested when, stony-faced, Indira neither cried nor discussed her brother's death. But Daisy knew guilt made her suffer more than any other member of her grief-stricken family and their close relatives.

"I'd do anything to help Indira, but I don't know how to," she muttered.

"I beg your pardon, what did you say?" Mum asked.

"I was thinking aloud."

"You know what that's the first sign of," Mum teased.

"Yes, the first sign of madness," Daisy muttered.

"Exactly. Now, finish your breakfast."

"I can't."

"All right, but make sure you eat properly at lunchtime."

"Okay. What are you going to do?"

"I'll ring the shop to tell them I can't come in today and I'll phone the doctor to arrange for her to visit Indira."

"Why?"

"For one thing, the poor girl has lost a lot of weight."

"How can her family be so cruel?" Daisy asked, unable to control herself. "They no longer drive her to and from to school, and-"

"Most children use the bus," Julia interrupted.

"Indira and I are not children. We are nearly fifteen."

Mum raised her eyebrows.

"Yes, I know most pupils travel on the bus, but you know what her family's like. They never liked her to be out on her own and-"

"I know-" Mum began.

"And now she has to cook most of the meals," Daisy broke in.

"Don't judge them, Daisy. I can't imagine how they feel. If something dreadful happened to you, I don't know how I could cope if you were murdered." Mum swallowed before she added, "Gopal was such a nice young man, kind, polite and respectful. I'm sure Indira misses him every day."

"She never talks about him."

"Not even to you?"

"Not really, mum. The Nathwanis are not like us, they don't discuss things. They merely get on with life."

"Kumud does not. You told me she spends most of her time in bed."

"Yes, she does."

"What time is it?" Mum glanced at the kitchen clock on the wall. "You'll be late if you miss the bus. Give the note to your school secretary to give to Miss Davidson. Off you go. Have a lovely day."

"And you." Daisy kissed her mum's cheek. "Bye."

"Goodbye, darling. Don't worry. We'll see what the doctor has to say and do everything we can to help Indira."

"What will you tell Dr Harris?"

"The truth, I'll tell her why Indira is staying at our house. Don't look so worried, Daisy, perhaps Indira's tears helped her. Sometimes we all need to let our hair down."

* * *

Strange to be at school without Indira. Daisy went into the office and handed Mum's notes to Mrs Lester and explained what was in them.

"Please wait here." Mum's letter in her hand, the secretary went into the office. Voices spoke quietly. She returned, leaving the door ajar. "Miss Davidson will see you now."

Why? Am I in trouble? Her footsteps slow, Daisy entered the office.

"Sit down, Daisy. Don't look so apprehensive, you've nothing to be anxious about."

Yes, I have, I'm worried about Indira.

She sat and gazed at the petite lady who commanded her pupils' respect.

"I've read your mother's notes. I hope Indira will soon return to school."

Daisy wriggled on the hard seat of the chair that faced the large desk. What did Mum explain in her note?

"After Indira's brother died, I told her she would always be welcome to see me if there's anything she wants to talk to about," Miss Davidson said.

Daisy continued to gaze at her headmistress' kind expression and believed she wanted to help Indira.

Miss Davidson cleared her throat. "Is there anything you'd like to tell me which can help your friend?"

Her cheeks hot, Daisy rearranged the position of her feet on the gleaming parquet floor. She and Indira trusted each other not to repeat secret conversations. "No, no, I can't think of anything. My mum's looking after Indira. I expect she told you in her note."

"Yes, she did. You may go Daisy," Miss Davidson said gently.

As though her headmistress was a queen, Daisy had the ridiculous impulse to curtsy. Mrs Lester gave her a note which explained why she was late to give to her teacher.

She ambled down the corridor toward her classroom. Miss Davidson's strict but she's not unkind like a couple of sarcastic teachers.

Worried about her best friend, the day dragged by without her. Several girls asked why Indira wasn't at school. A few wanted to question her about the murder.

"I'm very sorry for her. I'd cry buckets full of tears if my brother were killed," Sharon said while they ate lunch in the dining hall.

"Do you know a fifth form girl's brother and his friends bullied Indira and he was responsible for what's his names death?" Helena asked.

Daisy wanted to escape but couldn't leave until a teacher gave permission for all the girls to. She pushed her food around her plate with a fork. When news of Gopal's death spread, whispers and stares became Indira's companions. How would she have coped if she'd been unpopular? If friends hadn't told her how sorry they were and tried to shield her from the worst comments and gossip. Thank goodness Indira wasn't at school today, embarrassed by curiosity and pity.

Time seemed to pass slowly. Daisy couldn't pay attention. Her thoughts were with Indira during the French and English literature lessons. She struggled with a test on irregular verbs and Shakespeare's Julius Caesar didn't interest her. When the bell rang at the end of the school day, she hurried out of the building, ran up the drive to the main gate and down the road. She reached the bus stop in time to catch the early bus.

Chapter Twelve

Daisy walked the short distance from the bus stop to her house. She entered it very quietly in case her friend was asleep, but Indira sat on a stool at the kitchen table talking to Mum, who measured porridge oats.

"Are you making flapjacks?" she asked.

"Yes." Mum picked up the tin of golden syrup. "How was school today?"

"Good," Daisy prevaricated. "Shall I make tea?"

"Yes, please." Mum put butter and syrup in a saucepan to melt it.

Daisy filled the kettle with water and plugged it in. She glanced at her friend who had dark circles under her large eyes. "Are you okay, Indira?"

"Yes, I like it here."

Daisy assembled tea bags, milk, sugar, mugs, plates, and the cake tin, as she spoke to Indira, who looked exhausted. "I'm surprised that your father said you may stay here. Your family didn't allow you to spend even a night here before-" she broke off, miserably aware that if Indira hadn't run away because she wanted to spend

Christmas with them, she believed Gopal would be alive.

"I phoned Bapuji at the warehouse, to make sure he and the rest of the family don't object to me putting up here," Indira said, her voice flat.

"And I spoke to Indira's aunt – the one who moved into Indira's home to help until Kumud is feeling better," Mum explained.

How long will Indira stay here? Daisy wondered before she fell asleep that night.

Mum entered the bedroom in the morning. "Breakfast is ready."

Indira opened her eyes. "Oh, you're ready for school, Daisy. Why didn't you wake me up? I'll be late for school."

"No, you won't," Mum said. "Yesterday, the doctor said you need rest. You're not going back to school until next week. Now, both of you come downstairs."

Indira followed Daisy to the kitchen. Instead of sitting down, she stared at the table laid with white china ringed with blue, cutlery, and at a vase of dahlias. What colour are the deities' garlands today? Who strung them? She put her elbows on the table and propped her head on her hands.

"What's wrong?" Mrs Royston asked.

"I'm not myself. My head's swimming and I'm dizzy," Indira murmured.

"I think that's because of the sedatives the doctor prescribed for you to take last night. You'll feel all right after you've got some food inside you," Mrs Royston said.

"I am hungry," Indira admitted.

"Eat something. Doctor's orders." Mrs Royston's smile softened her abrupt words.

Indira sat. Daisy gave her a bowl of muesli.

Mrs Royston handed her a mug full of milky tea. "Don't stand on ceremony, Indira. you may call me Julia."

"Thank you, Mrs. Roy…"

"Julia," prompted Daisy's mum.

Indira blushed and whispered, "Julia."

It didn't seem respectful to call Daisy's mum by her first name. Indira folded her hands together and bent her head before she silently offered her food to Lord Krishna.

"That's nice," Julia said. "These days, few people say grace." Her forehead wrinkled. "After my mother died, Daisy and I slipped out of the habit."

Indira didn't pause to explain that she wasn't saying grace.

"Please, turn on the television, Daisy, I want to hear the weather forecast," Julia said.

Daisy switched on the portable television on the pine dresser, sat down and quickly finished her breakfast. "I'll be late if I don't get a move on." She kissed her mother's cheek. "Bye Mum, bye Indira."

"Bye, darling, have a nice day."

The front door opened. Outside, stirred by a rush of fresh air, the camel bells that hung from a hook tinkled. Each unfamiliar sound jangled Indira's nerves. She shouldn't be here sitting opposite Julia. She should either be going to school or helping Dada serve their deities, but she didn't want to go home because her family believed that if she had not run away on Christmas Eve, Gopal would be alive. And, regardless of karma, they were right. How could she bear the guilt for the rest of her life?

***

Indira put her hand over her mouth to conceal a yawn.

"If you're tired, go back to bed, Sweetie. The doctor said you need a week's rest."

"You're very kind."

"Another cup of tea, Indira?" Julia asked after Daisy went to school.

"Yes, please." Indira mumbled because her tongue felt too big for her mouth.

"The doctor also said people react differently to... to tragedies. I'm sure your family love you. I think they'll be as affectionate as they used to be when they've come to terms with their grief."

"Maybe, but it's almost nine months since my brother left his body," said Indira, too worn out to explain a son's importance in an Indian family.

Julia's blue eyes, the same shade as Daisy's, looked intently at her. "Sweetie, my doctor also provides professional help for your family, particularly for your mother. Lying in bed all day won't help her."

"I know. Bapuji, Dada, Kaka, and Kaki have tried to persuade her to-" Indira broke off afraid she might not be able to prevent tears.

Julia walked around the table and patted Indira's back. She rested her head against Daisy's mum and sniffed. "I'm sorry for being a nuisance."

"You're no trouble. I've loved you since you and Daisy became friends when you were four years old." Julia sat down opposite her. "Sweetie, I understand if you blame yourself for your brother's death and your family think you are guilty."

Indira's fists clenched. "How can you?"

Julia sipped tea and studied before she spoke. "Oliver, Daisy's dad, made a drama out of every cold, little ache, or pain. When he complained of stomach aches instead of encouraging him to consult the doctor, I told him not to make a fuss about nothing." Tears in her eyes, Julia continued. "Gradually, I realised Oliver wasn't making a mountain out of a molehill." She swallowed and clasped her mug with both hands as though the warmth comforted her heart. "When our doctor examined him, he immediately had him admitted to hospital as an emergency. Three months later my darling, good-natured Oliver died."

"That's dreadful," Indira said jerked out of her self-pity.

"Yes, it was. For months I held myself responsible for not sympathising with him when his stomach started to hurt. I didn't pay attention to how little he ate at home and told him not to stuff himself with unhealthy snacks at work." Julia gulped. "Too late for treatment, he told me he had starved himself to reduce the pain, but he had believed me when I told him not to make such a to do about a bit of pain. Eventually my mother, God bless her, talked sense into me, saying I was not responsible for Oliver's death. She explained he was too afraid of the diagnosis to make an appointment to consult the doctor." Julia wiped her eyes and drank more tea. "And you, Indira, are not solely responsible for Gopal's death."

"I am, if only I hadn't lost my temper with Kaka and Kaki and run away, he would be alive."

"If only are two of the saddest words in the world after a minor or major calamity. I am also guilty. If I hadn't invited you to spend Christmas with us, you would not have forgotten the park might be a dangerous place at night. If only you had been allowed to accept my invitation, you would have been at our house instead of outdoors. And if only you weren't shocked because your uncle drinks beer and alcohol and he and your aunt eat eggs, things would have been different. Your father, and uncle should have used force to stop you leaving the house, and they should have helped search for you as well as Gopal, may he rest in peace."

Every word struck a chord in her lacerated heart and tortured mind. "Thank you, Julia. I never thought about all that. I only blamed myself for the part I played."

"I know, but I found the strength to accept my darling Oliver's death. You must be strong and accept Gopal's. He loved you and wouldn't want you not to accept it during the rest of your life."

Since her brother's death, Indira went to bed exhausted, tormented by self-reproach and grief, and woke several times every night. Each time she stared into the dark and struggled to sleep. She put her hand over her mouth and yawned.

"You're tired," Julia said. "Back to bed with you. Sleep tight."

In the bathroom, Indira washed her face, rinsed her mouth, then settled beneath the covers on the sofa bed. Julia was right. Gopal wouldn't want her to be burdened with guilt. And because he spoke The Lord's name as he left his body, he was at peace with Him in his beautiful, eternal abode.

Daisy's lovely mum entered the bedroom. A hot water bottle tucked under her arm, she carried a tray which she put on the bedside table. "In case you're thirsty later, there's a jug of orange juice and a glass, and there's a glass of milk and a plate of biscuits for your elevenses. Is there anything else I may fetch for you?"

Indira struggled to keep her eyes open. "No, thank you."

Julia handed her the hot water bottle. "After I finish the housework, I'm going to the shops. Will you be all right on your own in the house until I come back and make our lunch?"

"Yes, please don't worry, Mrs. R...Julia, I'll be fine, I'll probably sleep all morning. Thank you for being so kind. Everything you said makes sense." She hugged the hot water bottle.

Julia kissed her cheek. "Sweetie, I think of you as a second daughter so there's no need to thank me."

Alone Indira drifted into sleep and slept soundly until lunchtime, as though she really was Julia's daughter, without any problems.

* * *

After Julia hurried to leave on time not to be late for work on Saturday, Indira sat at the table in the kitchen. The house was too quiet for her to concentrate, so she pushed away her geography textbook.

In the past her home would have been filled with familiar, reassuring sounds that added to her sense of security. Men's voices after work and at the weekend. Ba and Kaki's conversations, when their bangles tinkled as they gesticulated. A hand bell ringing or the recitation of prayers from the temple room. The sound of the front door that opened to admit family or friends and the rise and fall of voices in either Gujarati or English.

Once, someone would have asked her if she wanted a drink, and a hand would have patted her back or stroked her head while she studied, and people used to come in and out of the room. Today she would welcome the constant attention, an expression of love she had resented.

A rush of more unwanted tears stung her eyes. I'm being silly. It hasn't been like that at home for almost ten months. I must get used to it and help Dada to worship the deities. Indira rested her elbows on the table and pressed her face onto the palms of her hands. Perhaps things will improve now that Ba's sister Janavi Masie is living there. Even if she fusses and grumbles, a little, she'll be nice to me and help Ba.

Indira pulled her history book across the table, opened it, and read about Germany's invasion of Poland. Instead of concentrating as she read, she thought about her loss. She licked her dry lips. I'm stupid. Julia showed me how to accept it, but it's difficult. It is as though Gopal's always nearby. When I look at a door, I expect him to enter the room. She got up, washed her hands and face, wiped them on a paper towel and filled a glass with orange juice. If Daisy was awake, she might like some.

Indira rapped on the bedroom door. No answer. She rapped louder. When no reply came, Indira opened the door and saw Daisy lying tummy down, her feet waving in the air in time to the music on the radio.

"Good morning, Daisy," she said her voice louder than the music.

"Good morning." Daisy turned down the volume.

"I thought you might be thirsty, so I brought you a glass of orange juice."

"Thank you, I fancy some." Daisy turned over and sat up and took the glass. "I must get ready to take Mrs Bedmond's dog for a walk. Would you like to join us?"

"No thank you, I must study."

Daisy pouted. "You know the saying all work and no play makes Jack a dull boy, or should I say makes Indira a dull girl?"

Indira laughed, closed the door, and returned to the kitchen to drink orange juice at the breakfast bar. She read a paragraph twice without absorbing the content. Her mind drifted. She had thought she knew Daisy and her mum as well as she knew her own family, but she didn't. While staying with them she found out Julia often went out in the evenings to play bingo or go to the pub. Poor Daisy. When I'm not here she's left on her own. She has more freedom than I do, but I don't envy her. I was never alone at home.

Her tummy rumbled. She could almost taste the meals Ba and Kaki cooked. I don't like most of the food here. Chips or jacket potatoes with baked beans, tinned soup, and other uninteresting meals when Julia is too tired to cook, and Daisy serves something convenient.

Her cheeks burned. She shouldn't criticise and be ungrateful. Daisy's mum did the best she could.

On Sunday morning Julia slept later than usual and Daisy took the dog for its daily walk. Indira read two scenes in Julius Caesar and wrote answers to the questions at the back of the book. Enough studying today, which Julia called a day of rest. There was nothing on television Indira wanted to watch. Instead of cauliflower cheese with roast potatoes, defrosted peas, and gravy, which Julia planned, Indira decided to prepare lunch.

She didn't have all the spices she needed but there were enough that Ba had given Julia, for a curry made with cauliflower, peas, and potato. Instead of chapatis or parathas they could eat it with toast, and homemade lemon pickle Ba gave Julia. What about dessert? Oh, she could serve sweet rice.

"Something smells very tasty," remarked Julia coming into the kitchen, a warm dressing gown over her nightdress.

"I hope you don't mind me making curry for lunch, Mrs.... I mean.... Julia," Indira said, anxious in case she did.

"Of course, I don't. I'm grateful to you because I will have more time to enjoy my day off. When Mrs Cuthbert, who owns the greeting card shop, employed me before my mother died, she wanted me to work on Sundays. I refused because we always took

Daisy to church. Now, I need one lazy day a week."

"Of course, you do. I'll wash up, put everything away and clean the kitchen."

"Daisy can help you." Julia put the kettle on. "By the way, where is Daisy?"

"Walking that dog."

"Good, I don't know how Mrs Bedmond would cope with the animal if Daisy didn't help her. While she's out I hope she'll buy The Mail on Sunday for me." Julia looked at the kitchen clock. "Half-past eleven. I have slept late, but I'm not getting any younger and need to catch up on my sleep on Sundays."

Julia wouldn't need to catch up on her sleep if, on two or three nights out of seven, she didn't come home so late after playing bingo or meeting friends in the pub or a restaurant.

"Julia."

"Yes."

"I've been thinking."

Julia yawned, put a tea bag in a mug, poured boiling water into it, stirred it, and added milk and sugar. "What did you think?"

"That I should return home."

"I see."

"You have been so kind and -"

Julia chuckled. "Daisy and I enjoy having you here. How many times must I tell you to stop thanking me and saying I'm kind?"

Indira flapped her hands and did not know what to say.

"If you're sure you want to go home, pack your bags and I'll take you there this afternoon."

"Thank you."

"And Indira."

"Yes?"

"Whatever happens in the future, you will always be welcome here."

"Thank you," Indira repeated and hugged her. School and helping at home would keep her busy on weekdays, but if things didn't improve after she returned, she would spend the weekends here.

Chapter Thirteen

Daisy entered the kitchen after her walk in the park, where she avoided the area near the pond where Gopal died. "Good morning," she greeted her mum who sat at the small table opposite Indira.

Mum looked up from her late breakfast, grilled mushrooms and tomatoes on toast. "How is Mrs Bedmond?"

"She seemed okay. As usual she thanked me several times for walking Rascal. On my way home, I stopped at the corner shop and bought this for you." She put The Mail on Sunday, filled with supplements on the table.

"Thank you, darling. Did you have breakfast before you left?"

"Yes, but I'm hungry again." Daisy poured milk into a glass, fetched the biscuit tin, and put two digestive biscuits covered with plain chocolate and a couple of custard creams on a small plate. She sniffed. "Something smells nice."

Mum smiled. "Yes, it does. Don't eat too much, you need room for lunch which Indira was kind enough to make. That's why I'm not eating much."

"Oh, I can't wait to try it. Indira' a good cook. I'm sure it will be delicious." She decided not to add ginger biscuits to her plate and put the lid back on the biscuit tin.

"Have you packed your bags, Indira?" Mum asked as she studied the T.V. guide for the week in a supplement.

"Not yet. It won't take long. I didn't bring much with me." Indira stood. "I'll do it now."

"Pack!" Daisy followed Indira into the hall.

"Yes, I've bothered you and your mum for long enough, and I think you'll be glad to have your room to yourself."

"Don't be silly. I enjoy sharing it with you. And Mum said you may stay for as long as you want to."

"Yes, I know. She's very kind but it's time for me to leave."

"You ran away because –" Daisy didn't want to upset her friend, so she broke off for a moment. "I won't go into that, but why are you returning?"

""I'm worried about Dada, and I miss our deities."

"But-"

"Don't fret about me. My aunt, my mother's sister, is at home. She's taking care of Mum. Things will improve."

"I hope so."

"So do I." Indira smiled to reassure her friend.

Daisy rolled her eyes. "I'll miss you."

"Don't be silly, we'll see each other at school every day and can visit each other at the weekends."

"I know, but it won't be the same. Since you came here, it's been as though I have a sister."

Indira hugged her. "Being such good friends is the next best thing. We might have been blood sisters in a previous birth and that's why we're so fond of each other."

"Maybe," replied Daisy.

"It's possible. Don't you believe in reincarnation? Dada and I explained that when the body dies our soul passes into a new one."

"I'm not sure, although it's more logical than either my grandmother's conviction that heaven and ever-lasting hell exist, or mum's belief that we only have one life, so we might as well make the most of it and enjoy it while we can."

Indira put her suitcase on the bed.

Daisy sighed as she helped her to fold clothes and pack them.

Indira put aside her peacock blue silk sari, blouse, and cotton petticoat.

Daisy stroked the soft silk. "Are you going to wear those today?"

"Yes, I'll change into them before I go home." Indira caught her lower lip between her teeth.

"Is something wrong?"

Indira winced and let go of her lip. "Not really, I only wondered if ... no ... it doesn't matter."

"What doesn't matter?"

"I was thinking about Scarlet. Does she know Gopal left his body? How much did she know about him?" Indira raised her eyebrows and folded and refolded her school skirt. "Suppose she doesn't know where he lived and can't find out why he doesn't visit her." Indira grimaced. "Oh! Why am I curious? It's not worth talking about. Even if Gopal wanted to marry her, my family would never have accepted her instead of an Indian girl."

Daisy looked sideways at her. "Even if that's true, if Gopal loved her, she must be nice. She should be told what happened to him." Daisy scratched an itchy spot on her arm. "But, perhaps she does, his name and photo were reported in some newspapers."

"You're right." Indira put her toilet bag, comb, and hairbrush into the suitcase.

"Have you mentioned her to your parents?" Daisy asked, unable to restrain her curiosity.

"No. I should have burned her letter and the photos so they would never see them." The suitcase closed, Indira shook her head. "I don't know why I hid them."

"You should give them to your father and mother."

"Why? Things were bad enough when I came here without them finding out about my brother and his girlfriend."

Daisy tutted. "Indira, it's not fair."

She didn't answer until she fastened the suitcase, picked it up and stood it near the door. "What isn't fair?"

"Your parents and your aunt and uncle treat you like a criminal. They think Gopal was perfect. He wasn't, no one is."

"I don't want to talk about him," Indira shouted,

"I'm sorry. I only thought- "Daisy faltered. "I remembered your grandfather telling me people should be honest because, if they aren't, it's like grappling with a ghost. There's nothing substantial."

Mum entered the room. "What's going on? Why did one of you shout?"

"I told Indira to tell her family about Scarlet. I think they should know the truth about Gopal," Daisy blurted, shocked by Indira's anger.

"Who is Scarlet and what is the truth?" her mother asked.

Indira sank onto the edge of the bed and covered her face with her hands. "Daisy, why did you mention her to your mother? You promised not to tell anyone about her," she mumbled through her fingers.

"To tell what?" Mum sat beside Indira and put an arm around her.

Indira removed her hands from her face. "Daisy, I'm sorry for shouting at you."

"And I apologise for mentioning Scarlet."

"It's okay. I suppose secrets always come out." Indira gazed at Mum. "Before my brother left his body, Daisy and I found photos of him with a beautiful red-haired girl and a letter to him signed Scarlet."

Mum didn't seem to be shocked or surprised. "Sweetie, did you talk to your brother about your discovery?"

"No, I didn't have a chance to corner him in private," Indira whispered.

Daisy looked sympathetically at her. "We found the photos and the letter on the day we went with Gopal to cut holly. His mum told him to put his coat in the laundry basket in his room. Instead, Indira took it upstairs. Before she put it with his dirty clothes, she emptied the pockets. That's when she found them. And then... and then he died on Christmas Eve."

"Most young men have girlfriends. Indira, why haven't you told your parents about Gopal and Scarlet? They might want to meet her," Mum said.

"Believe me, they wouldn't, and I shouldn't have worried about her."

Daisy guessed Indira tried to find words to explain how her parents would react. "It's a bit awkward, Mum. Indira's family wouldn't approve of Scarlet and Gopal's ...um... affair. They wouldn't understand if, like you and Dad, Gopal or Indira chose free love instead of marriage."

"And I don't believe in promiscuity. Your father and I were totally committed to each other. If Oliver had lived, I'm sure we would never have split up. A marriage certificate couldn't have made us either love each other or you more than we did." Mum dabbed her eyes with a handkerchief. "Indira, your family have as much right to their opinions as I have, and come to think of it, Gopal and Scarlet might have been so deep in love that it would have endured, but I'll say no more about it. I'll have a bath and get ready to enjoy lunch."

* * *

While Daisy set the pine table in the dining room, Indira made toast, heated the curry and sweet rice then offered it to Lord Krishna. She carried the meal to the small, but elegant room with cream walls and two large mirrors that made it appear more spacious. She put the hot dishes on place mats to prevent them marking the table that Julia found in a secondhand furniture shop, as well as six pine chairs and a sideboard. A crystal vase, bought from a car boot or charity shop, filled with fragrant yellow roses from the bush by the front door, stood on the center of the table.

"Mum's reading the newspaper in the lounge. I'll tell her lunch is ready."

"I hope you'll enjoy this," Indira said when they sat at table. "I try my best, but I'm not as good a cook as either Ba or Kaki." She watched Julia eat her first mouthful. "Is the curry all right? Before I cook, I always worry because I might put too much or too little salt or the spices aren't quite right."

Daisy ate a piece of bread and curry. "It's yummy."

"Yes, it is," Julia agreed. "Indira, if it's not too much trouble, I'd like you to teach me how to cook this when you visit us again."

"Not a problem," she said, too nervous about what would happen at home to eat much.

"I'd also like to learn how to make that soup...what-is-it called?" Julia asked.

"Dahl," Indira said. "I'll bring lentils and the other ingredients, to show you how to make it."

Julia smiled at Daisy. "Darling, you should join us if you would like to learn."

Indira looked down at her plate. Lucky Daisy. Julia gave her chores and rarely asked her to do anything extra. Julia wouldn't scold Daisy if she refused to share the cooking lessons. She wished she had the same freedom of choice at home instead of being told to obey if she said she didn't want to do something.

"Some more sweet rice, Julia?"

Julia patted her stomach. "No, thank you. I really enjoyed the delicious meal, but I couldn't eat another mouthful. Daisy and I will clear up, then I'll read the paper until three o'clock when I'll drive you home."

Indira stacked the dirty plates and bowls. She glanced affectionately at Julia. "I'll help Daisy while you sit down."

* * *

Indira and Daisy sat in the lounge where, instead of reading the newspaper, Julia had drifted off to sleep. At four o'clock she opened her eyes and looked at them sleepily.

"I'll make you a cup of tea, Mum."

"Thank you, darling." Julia looked at the clock on the mantlepiece. "Goodness, look at the time. Indira, after I drink the tea, I'll drive you to your house."

At a quarter to five, Indira got into the car with Daisy, and Julia, who had refreshed her make up and tidied her hair. Fifteen minutes later Julia parked the car.

Indira got out and stared apprehensively at the sash windows. She was sure Dada would be pleased to see her and Massie would welcome her. How would her parents, aunt and uncle react? Had they missed her?

"Come on, Indira." Daisy took the suitcase and school bag out of the boot.

"Sweetie don't forget my door's always open for you. Come and have a natter or stay with us whenever you want to."

"Thank you for the invitation, Julia." Indra hesitated then added, "Although you don't like me thanking you, I must repeat that I am grateful to for everything you've done for me."

"My pleasure. Come along." Julia went to the front door and rang the bell. By the time the girls entered the porch, the door – secured by a safety chain – opened a little.

"What do you want?" a woman asked.

Indira recognised her voice. "Kaki, it's me, Indira."

"What are you doing here?"

"I've come home, please open the door."

"No. You left, so you are not welcome. This house is no longer your home."

"What do you mean? Of course, it is." She pressed the doorbell." Let me in!"

"No. Your father won't take you back."

"Why not?"

"Are you stupid? Don't you know there's no place here for a daughter who has been sleeping away from home without her father's permission?"

Indira gasped. "I had his permission. I haven't done anything wrong. I stayed with my girlfriend and her mother."

"You should have been at home in your own bed."

"Julia can't keep me forever."

"That's not my problem. Mrs Royston shouldn't have encouraged you to run away from home."

Indira bit her lip.

Julia frowned. "I didn't encourage your niece to run away. When she arrived, Indira was in a terrible state because she was mistreated at home. I phoned her father, who gave permission for her to stay with us."

This real-life nightmare can't be happening. "Please let me in, I want to see Bapuji."

"He doesn't want to see you," Kaki said.

"I don't believe you." Julia rang the doorbell again.

Indira's shoulders slumped. "Stop ringing it, Julia, no matter what we say or do Kaki won't let us into the house."

"Yes, she will," Dada said. "Open the door," he ordered Kaki.

The chain clinked. The door opened wide.

Dada put his hand on her head to give her his blessing. "Welcome home, Indira, I think Sri Krishna and Srimati Radharani have missed you and look forward to wearing the beautiful flower garlands you make."

There was no one else in the world like her grandfather. She stooped to touch his feet, but he gently held her forearms and drew her upright.

"Look." Daisy pointed at a grey Morris Minor which drew up in the driveway next to Julia's car.

They watched a beautiful young woman emerge from it. She pointed at Indira. "I think you're Gopal's sister. He loved you very much and told me all about you."

Indira squared her shoulders. "Yes, I am," she said her voice choked with emotion.

"Hello, you don't know me. I'm –."

"We recognise you," Daisy interrupted. "Indira and I saw photos of you with Gopal."

Indira gazed at a determined dandelion that poked up through the gravel. "And my friend and I read your letter to Gopal." She stood still, her feet apart and her hands on her hips.

"Oh! Did he mention me to your family?" his girlfriend asked, her words rushed.

Worried about Dada's reaction, Indira glanced at him. "No, Scarlet, he didn't."

Chapter Fourteen

The Nathwanis clustered in the porch within hearing distance of Scarlet, and Julia stood with Daisy on the wide steps in front of the house and heard a baby crying.

Scarlet rushed to her car and took out an infant and a baby bag.

Followed by Daisy, Julia hurried to her and peered at the little one. "Is your beautiful baby a boy or a girl?"

"A boy. Gopal would have loved him and been as proud of him as I am," Scarlet replied, a defiant note in her voice and her eyes moist.

"What is his name?" Julia asked.

"Ah, a good question. Please let me explain how I chose it." She scrutinised the Nathwani's faces. "When I became pregnant, Gopal told me the baby could hear everything, so he read the Ramayana to us." Scarlet looked down at her son. "When I wanted to choose a name for our son or daughter, Gopal explained that the precise time of a baby's birth should be noted so an astrologer could choose the correct initial for it." She continued to stare at the Nathwanis. "To honour the custom, I consulted an

Indian astrologer who said it should begin with L. Daisy, Mrs Royston, I chose Lakshman, the name of Rama's younger brother."

"That's a lovely name," Daisy said. "I watched the film with Indira. Lakshman drew a circle around Sita, his sister-in-law, to protect her, but she stepped out of it and Ravana captured her. I have a video of the film. If you would like to, you may borrow it," Daisy said while Mum gazed at Lakshman.

"Thank you, Daisy. I would like that."

"Perhaps Scarlet would like you to hold the baby bag for her," Julia suggested.

"Yes, of course." Daisy took it from her.

Julia looked at Scarlet. "I understand the terrible time you've been through. Daisy's father died when she was very young. But I have her and you've got this little angel. May I hold him?"

Scarlet put Lakshman in Julia's arms. "Yes, I've lost Gopal, but I'm grateful because I have our son and my parents adore him."

"Come here, Indira," Bapuji ordered.

She turned around and took a few steps toward the house.

Scarlet caught hold of her arm. "Please wait for a moment. I came here to give you and your family an opportunity to meet Lakshman, but I'm very nervous. Would you introduce me to them?"

Lakshman grizzled. Immediately Scarlet took him from Julia and spoke softly to him.

Her back toward Scarlet, Indira hesitated. If her brother hadn't become involved with Scarlet, she wouldn't have run away from the house on Christmas Eve and Gopal would be alive. As soon as she thought that she looked at Dada, who stood on the top step in front of her parents, aunts, and uncle, always tranquil because he applied their religion and philosophy to daily life regardless of what happened. If she blamed Scarlet for Gopal leaving his body, she would be as bad as her parents, Kaka, and Kaki, who held her responsible for Gopal's murder. But as Dada had explained, karma was very complicated so she must not blame herself. As soon as her thought took shape, her understanding of Dada increased. He was serene because he depended on Krishna and applied His words in the Bhagavadgita. She should do her best to follow his example.

"Indira, when I came here, I hoped we could be friends."

Tongue-tied, assaulted by emotion, Indira could not say a word as she scrutinised Scarlet's beautiful face, with high cheek bones, a straight nose, arched eyebrows, and beautiful moss green eyes.

"If you won't come with me, I'll go to the house with Lakshman," Scarlet continued.

"Please don't. I'm sure my parents won't welcome you, and my aunt and uncle will reject you. If you force yourself on them, who knows what effect it might have on Dada, who has a weak heart."

Scarlet drew Lakshman a little closer and walked forward.

With Daisy beside her Indira followed Scarlet and Julia to the house where her family now clustered in front of it.

Dada gestured to his sons, daughters-in-laws, and Massie to step back. "Come in, Mrs Royston, Daisy and you, Scarlet."

As they stepped into the lounge, Daisy whispered to Indira. "Does your grandfather know? Is he angry?"

"I don't think so."

"Please be seated, Scarlet," Dada said.

She sat down on a wing chair next to the one Julia was sitting on, which faced a sofa on which Indira's Ba, Kaki and Massie sat. On a second sofa, set at right angles to the first, sat her Kaka and Bapuji.

"Indira, please fetch refreshments for our guests."

Daisy followed Indira into the kitchen. She closed the door and asked. "What's going to happen? Will they take you back?"

"I don't know."

"Why did your father tell your aunt not to let you into the house?"

"I never thought Bapuji would follow the custom of throwing out a daughter for staying away from home."

"Do you want to live at home?"

Indira twirled a strand of her loose, shoulder length hair round her thumb, thought for a minute and replied. "I don't know whether I want to live here or leave home and see what life brings."

"What do you think your father will have to say about Scarlet and her baby?"

"We'll have to wait and see," Indira answered as she made Indian style tea for her family and English tea for Daisy, Julia, and Scarlet.

"You're so calm, Indira."

"I'm not inside."

She picked up the tray, Daisy opened the door, and they returned to the lounge. As they entered the room, they heard Indira's Kaka shout. "No! We can't take Indira back. What would people say?"

Scarlet got up. "I'm going home."

"Go," Kaka said without looking at her.

"Please sit down again, Scarlet, Indira's brought tea for you," Dada said. She hesitated and Dada repeated. "Please sit down."

"Scarlet, how do you like your tea?"

"Milky without sugar, please, Indira."

Lakshman woke up when Indira handed his mother the tea. He kicked her arm. A few drops of the hot liquid fell onto his cheek. He screwed up his face and screamed repeatedly. Immediately, Ba, Kaki and Massie put aside their disapproval of Scarlet. They rushed toward her chair. Kaki scooped up the baby. Massie hurried out of the room to fetch an ointment to soothe the pain of the burn.

Kaka forgot to speak English and ordered his wife in Gujrati. "Put the little bastard down."

Kaki glared at Kaka, held the child more closely and patted his back. "He looks like his father did when he was a baby."

Indira offered Bapuji a mug of tea. His dark eyes scanned her face. For a moment she thought he would refuse to accept it. He took the mug and put it down on the coffee table.

"How could your brother have behaved so shamefully?" he asked, stood, and embraced her.

"I don't know, Bapuji."

Although she returned his hug, deep inside her she knew things would never again be as they were once. If she always obeyed him, he'd be affectionate otherwise he might disown her.

"Your brother's behaviour and secret marriage was shameful. I know you would not act dishonourably." He stood and embraced her.

Kaka looked furious. "Are you going to take Indira back after she went to the white woman and her daughter's house?"

"Racist!" Julia exclaimed. "Your family's cruelty drove Indira out of the house. You are a hypocrite. You follow your religion, but you are neither t-total or vegetarian, and you have no compassion for Scarlet or her son, who will never know his father."

"Please say no more about us," Scarlet said. "I only came here because I thought the family might want to see Lakshman."

"Why should we want to?" asked Kaka. "We're not interested in a bastard."

"A bastard!" shouted Scarlet. "How dare you use that word! It's not even politically correct! It's an insult! You are contemptible."

"Don't be upset, Scarlet, Mr N is not worth it," Julia said.

"I'm not. Let him think whatever he wants."

"You are, and I don't blame you, but when I was little Mum told me sticks and stones can break my bones, but words can never hurt me."

"Words can cut a person to the quick. And what makes him assume my son is-."

"Neither that woman and her baby, nor the English woman and her daughter should have been allowed to enter the house. As for Indira, she has forfeited her place in the family," Kaka raged.

"I hope you will forgive me if I speak plainly," said Julia.

Indira put her hand over her mouth to disguise her smile. Despite her mild tone of voice, if Julia were a dog her hair would bristle. Kaka scowled. Indira sank back into her chair and waited to hear what Julia, who was always forthright, would say.

"I'll come straight to the point. From now on all of you, except for Indira's grandfather and her mother's sister who have always treated Indira well, stop making Indira's life hell." The expression in her eyes hard, Julia stared at Ba. "Kumud, I hope you have stopped selfishly wallowing in bed. Take care of Indira, who mourns her brother's death as much as the rest of you. She is a daughter to be proud of and, as you found out, dear Gopal was not everything you believed him to be." Julia stood and straightened her back. "And you, Mr N are a racist and a hypocrite. You jabber about your culture, but you are neither t-total nor vegetarian, and you haven't got an ounce of compassion for Scarlet or her son, who will grow up without a father."

"Don't interfere, Mrs Royston. That woman knows we are wealthy. She's here for whatever she can get," Kaki said, venomous as a snake. She pointed at Scarlet. "Leave the house with your bastard."

"A bastard!" Scarlet shouted. "How dare you say that? I am Gopal's widow."

Bapuji and Ba studied Scarlet during silence as dark as death.

"I don't believe you," Kaka bellowed.

"I can prove my marriage is legal." Scarlet handed Lakshman to Julia. She fumbled with the clasp of her handbag to open it and pulled out a paper. "Examine this, if you don't believe me, it's my marriage certificate." She stood, gave it to Dada, took Lakshman from Julia and kissed his head.

"Gopal and Scarlet were married so-" Dada began.

"She must have set a honey trap for my poor nephew," Kaki interrupted him.

Kaka stared at Scarlet who nursed Lakshman at her breast, his head covered from sight by a shawl. "Am I the only sane person here?" he asked. "That woman couldn't have been married to Gopal by a brahmin priest. She and the child have no claim on us."

"Really!" Scarlet's sarcastic tone sounded like a gunshot. "We were also married by a brahmin priest at the Hare Krishna temple, Bhaktivedanta Manor, in Letchmore Heath. He will confirm it."

Ba sprang up. "Is it true? Indira, is it true? Is that baby my Gopal's son?" she asked and fainted with so little warning that Indira only managed to catch her in time to prevent her crashing onto the floor.

Bapuji knelt beside Ba his eyes so wide open that it looked as though they might pop out of his head. "Phone the doctor."

Julia stooped to check Ba's pulse. "Don't panic. Trust me, I completed a first aid course. Smelling salts will revive her." Julia hunted in her handbag for them. She unscrewed the top of a tiny green glass bottle and held it under Ba's nose.

Ba's eyelids fluttered.

Anxious, Indira watched Julia continue to hold the pungent contents under Ba's nose until she opened her eyes.

Ba spluttered and feebly pushed Julia's hand away.

"What happened? Why am I lying on the floor?"

The taut lines on Bapuji's face began to relax.

"You fainted, Pyari."

"Oh!" Ba tried to sit up. "I am dizzy."

"It will wear off. You need hot, sweet tea which helps after a shock," Julia said.

"I'll make some." Massie bustled out of the lounge.

Kaka ignored her, scowled. "And there's no place in this house for foreigners or Indira who ran away from home and-"

"You have said enough," Dada said to Kaka. He stood, the palms of his hands and fingertips pressed together. "Karma is as complicated as the roots of a banyan tree, and in kali yuga, it is difficult to understand dharma."

Daisy interrupted. "What do those words mean?"

Indira appreciated Dada's sweet smile at Julia. "I like your daughter. Only unintelligent people don't ask questions about that which they don't understand." He gazed at Daisy. "Kali yuga is the fourth and last age in which hypocrisy, lies and quarrels are prevalent." Dada closed his eyes for a second or two. "Dharma means duty, which we must observe. As head of this household, I must not shrink from mine." His eyes confronted Kaka, who shifted on his comfortable chair, then Kaki, who covered her head with the end of her pink silk sari.

"Scarlet," Dada said.

"Yes."

"Please give Lakshman to me."

She gave the baby to him.

Held in one arm, Dada touched Lakshman's head.

In response to the symbolic gesture, Indira released her breath.

"Scarlet, you and Lakshman are members of my family. I own the business which my sons manage and this house, and by right may decide who lives here. If you would like to, you may make your home here, learn about our way of life, and instruct your son so that he becomes part of his father's heritage. I think it is what Gopal would have wanted. You don't need to decide on the spur of the moment. Discuss my offer with your parents. If you refuse it, please visit us often. Whichever you choose, we will support you financially and set up a trust fund for Lakshman."

"I wouldn't live here with her and that-"

"Harish, be quiet. You have said enough." Dada said. "If you won't accept my decisions, you are free to leave with your wife."

Kaka gasped, bowed his head. "How could I leave you?"

Dada looked at Indira. "In future, if you wish to live at home, you must discuss your problems with us and all of us must advise you. Don't be nervous. I understand you have many choices in this country which you would not have had in India."

"I want to make the right choices, Dada."

"What do you want to do? Do you want to remain at home, serve the deities, continue your education and, one day, agree to a marriage that pleases you and your family, or want to leave home?"

Indira swallowed. "I...I want to live at home, but I don't want all of you to blame me for Gopal's death."

"I've not blamed you and now it's time for all of us to set grief aside." Indira looked at Dada. *He's like a calm eye in the center of a storm. For as long as I live, my memories of him and his unconditional love will inspire me.*

"Harish," Dada began, "you must leave my house for these reasons. You allowed your wife to cook food for Srimati Radharani and Sri Krishna when she was not a vegetarian, and neither of you see everyone equally, regardless of creed, economic situation, nationality, or race, which is unacceptable to Him." Dada's shoulders heaved. "Also, when you mistreated Indira, who is His devotee, you forgot that Sri Krishna will forgive an offence toward Himself but not to His devotee. For these reasons you must leave my house."

Kaka sprang up, prostrated himself before Dada, and clasped his feet. "I am sorry. Please don't cast me out."

"Don't apologise to me. Apologise to Lord Krishna and ask for His forgiveness. Also ask Indira, His devotee for her forgiveness."

Tears in his eyes, his cheeks flushed, Kaka stood. "Father-"

"I won't listen to your arguments or justification, but I shall always wish you and your wife well. You may visit us and discuss your future in my company with your brother at the office."

His shoulders slumped Kaka left the room with Kaki.

"Indira," Dada said when the door closed behind them.

"Yes, Dada?"

"What is it that you wish to do?"

Indira gazed at Bapuji but spoke to Dada. "When I leave school, I want to study at college or university then work for the Nathwani Company."

Dada observed Bapuji's reaction. "Govinda, we must look to the future. Indira's namesake is a wife, mother, and India's prime minister, so with our blessings our Indira may join our firm, marry and by Lord Krishna's mercy have children."

Bapuji's smile illuminated his face for the first time since her brother left his body. "Yes, she may, and her mother and I will be proud of her."

Daisy pulled her to her feet and hugged her. "I'm very happy for you, and we'll always be friends."

Everyone relaxed as though Daisy's comment freed the room from cobwebs.

"And we will always be pleased when you visit us and Indira visits you, even at Christmas," Dada looked from Daisy to Scarlet.

Scarlet's eyes glowed. "I understand why Gopal loved you so much. Would it be all right for me to visit you and your family and get to know you better before I decide whether to continue at university?"

Some of the usual strain left Ba's face, making her seem young and enthusiastic. "If you go to university, I could help you to look after Lakshman and cook for you if you enjoy our vegetarian food."

"Yes, I do. My parents are Buddhists who brought me up to be a vegetarian. It's one of the things which Gopal and I appreciated about each other."

A smile replaced Bapuji's frown. "Welcome to our family, Scarlet."

"Thank you," Scarlet said,

"Ah," Ba breathed. "We have a daughter-in-law and a grandson."

Scarlet smiled at Ba. "Would you like to hold Lakshman?"

Joy illuminated Ba's face as she held out her arms. Her grandson snug on her lap she quietly sang a Gujarati lullaby to him.

"Scarlet," Dada commenced, "take as much time as you need to decide but bear in mind that one day, if Lakshman is to manage my business with Indira he must be trained.

But whatever he decides, he will share half of his father's inheritance with her. We'll speak about this on another occasion. It's time for me to prepare everything for evening worship."

"Thank you. It's time for me to leave," Scarlet said.

"Before you go, there's one more thing for me to say."

"What?"

"You may call me Dada."

Scarlet wiped away a few tears that glistened on her cheeks.

"Come on, Daisy," Julia said. "It's time for us to go home."

Dada smiled. "Thank you for taking such good care of Indira. This year Daisy must spend Diwali with us and – if you invite her – Indira may spend Christmas with you."

"I think you're wonderful," Daisy said to Dada.

The End

Bibliography

Bhagavad Gita As It Is translated by His Divine Grace A. C. Bhaktivedanta Swami Prabhupada

Ramayana: India's immortal tale of Adventure, Love and Wisdom by Krishna Dharma.

The International Society of Krishna Consciousness' worldwide temples, farms etc.

https://centres.iskcon.org

Indira's Recipe for Cauliflower, peas and potato curry.

2 inches (6cms) grated ginger.

1 dessert spoon (4 ml) black mustard seeds.

4 tablespoons ghee, olive oil or butter.

4 medium sized potatoes cut into half inch cubes.

6 ounces of fresh or frozen peas.

1 medium size cauliflower cut into small florets.

1 pound (230 grams) chopped tomatoes or a 230 gram tin chopped tomatoes.

1 dessert spoon (4ml) of turmeric.

1 tablespoon (40 ml) ground coriander.

1 tablespoon (40 ml) ground cumin.

1 dessert spoon (4ml) garam masala (mixed spice.) Optional.

1 dessert spoon (4 ml) white or brown sugar.

1 dessert spoon (4 ml) salt.

2 tablespoons (90 ml) finely chopped coriander or parsley.

Fresh or powered chilli to taste. Optional.

Heat the ghee, oil or butter add the mustard seeds. When they crackle add the fresh chilli – optional - dry spices, salt, and sugar. Stir the mixture over a low heat until it is a paste. Add the vegetables and stir until they are coated with the spices. Stir in the tomatoes. Cook over a low heat, stirring the curry occasionally until the vegetables are soft. If necessary, add a little water to prevent the vegetables sticking to the bottom of the saucepan. Stir in the fresh coriander or parsley.

Serve with chapatis or paratha and, or, rice.

Indira's Rice Pudding

¼ cup (120 ml) rice cooked.
1 tablespoon (20ml) butter.
Half cup (60 ml) sugar.
4 cups (1 liter) fresh whole milk.
¼ cup (20ml) currants or seedless raisins.
Seeds from four pods of cardamon. Optional.

Bring the milk and butter to the boil in a saucepan. Add the cooked rice and continuously stir the mixture making sure it doesn't stick to the saucepan for five minutes. Add the currants or seedless raisins and stir for another five minutes. (The rice pudding should thicken and be creamy. If not, stir for another two or three minutes.) Remove the saucepan from the heat and stir in the sugar. Refrigerate the pudding. If it becomes too thick, stir in a little cold milk.

Rosemary Morris's novels published by BWL Publishing Inc.

Regency
Sunday's Child
Monday's Child
Tuesday's Child
Wednesday's Child
Thursday's Child
Friday's Child
Saturday's Child
False Pretences

Early 18th Century
Tangled Love
Far Beyond Rubies
The Captain and The Countess
The Viscount and The Orphan

Medieval
Yvonne, Lady of Cassio
Grace, Lady of Cassio

Rosemary Morris lives in a town in Southeast England with easy access to London and open countryside.

At heart Rosemary is a historian. Her novels which have received many five-star reviews, are sensual but with firmly closed bedroom doors so the reader can relish the details of emerging romances.

When Rosemary is not engrossed researching historical non-fiction, studying Indian classical literature, she is reading fiction, writing, or engaged in 'writerly' activities. She enjoys time spent with her family and friends, knitting, growing her own in her organic garden, and putting it to good use in her vegetarian cuisine.

Rosemary enjoys contact with her readers. Her e-mail address is: srilekharach@hotmail.com

www.ingramcontent.com/pod-product-compliance
Lightning Source LLC
Chambersburg PA
CBHW051431290426
44109CB00016B/1506